LP

THE CHRISTIAN ENCOUNTERS

THE
NEW
LEISURE

RUDOLPH F. NORDEN

CONCORDIA
PUBLISHING
HOUSE
SAINT LOUIS

Concordia Publishing House, St. Louis, Missouri

Concordia Publishing House Ltd., London, W. C. 1

© 1965 Concordia Publishing House

Library of Congress Catalog Card No. 65-16961

Manufactured in the United States of America

PREFACE

This brief study is based on three assumptions. First, it is assumed that readers who desire to join the author in exploring this topic in the Christian Encounter Series are Christians. Christians are people who in faith and life are committed to Jesus Christ. In their explicit and implicit confession they acknowledge Him as Son of God, Savior, and Lord of their lives. Christians meeting together over the pages of this book bring such commitment to the discussion at hand. They expect the matter to be treated from a point of view distinctly Christian. This modest volume reflects the Christian viewpoint and is thus different from secular books available on the subject.

A second assumption in the writing of a Christian Encounter book is that the subject impinge sufficiently on the borderline of Christian and mundane life as to involve a great many people. There has to be something — an issue, a problem, a movement — in the world at large which Christians encounter. In this instance the issue is leisure, leisure as it affects people working shorter hours, people retiring at an earlier age, and the like. At this time we do not as yet fully know what changes the automation revolution will bring. Nevertheless, leisure is a factor in American life to which much thought must be given. The author hopes that this presentation will introduce readers to the problems and opportunities of the new leisure. For him it was a happy experience to give of his leisure to write on leisure.

Given, on the one hand, a Christian people and, on the other, a problem in the world, it is our third assumption that there be an encounter, a face-to-face confrontation, a meeting of minds. Obviously, were Christians to run away from public affairs or to consider them only in their own enclaves, there could be no encounter. When they forthrightly take note of happenings in the world, study and read about them, join with representatives of the public in open dialog, and bring their spiritual insights to bear on the solution, then there is encounter. The willingness of Christian people to participate in community and national questions is one of the most encouraging developments of our time. It augurs well for both church and nation.

RUDOLPH F. NORDEN

THE SIX CHAPTERS

1

THE NEW
LEISURE IN AMERICA TODAY

America must brace itself for a way of life in which leisure is a factor of mounting importance. The first shock waves of a social revolution bringing more free time to more people are already being felt. Many are experiencing the effects firsthand; more will do so in the future. Hardly a day goes by but that discussions, in private and in public, direct attention to the new leisure as a phase of explosive changes shaking American society. For better or for worse, "the new age of leisure is one of the realities of American life," according to Max Kaplan in *Leisure in America: A Social Inquiry.*

If the new leisure trend is a reality, to what extent is it a revolutionary one? Staggering predictions are the order of the day. Some social scientists foresee the time, perhaps in the next 25 or even 10 years, when people constituting 2 percent of our population can do the necessary work to provide food and consumer goods for the remaining 98 percent; when state governments will establish departments of leisure to balance departments of labor; when public schools will be required to teach courses in leisure skills, the fourth R thus added to the traditional triad of Reading, 'Riting, and 'Rithmetic standing for "Rest." Looking farther into the future, Dr. Marion Clawson, a Government administrator and economist, holds that A. D. 2000 Americans will have 660 billion more hours of leisure than in 1950. Others, of course, are more conservative in their forecasts. All agree that the age of more uncommitted time is here.

The new leisure of the latter half of the 20th century is different from anything human society has experienced in all its history. To be sure, previous cultures and civilizations harbored leisure classes. A considerable community of noble-born, nonworking persons flourished, for example, in ancient Greece. It consisted of the political, social, and cultural elite who turned labor activities over to slaves and people of lower classes to be at liberty to serve the state. Oliver Goldsmith's lines from *The Travveller* come to mind in this connection:

For just experience tells, in every soil,
That those who think must govern those that toil.

Philosophers, too, were members of this leisure group. Aristotle held, so Josef Pieper declares in his classical *Leisure the Basis of Culture,* that "leisure is the centrepoint about which everything revolves." Consequently, let men of wisdom not debase themselves by doing menial work, but let them engage in the nobler leisure activity of reflection. Writes W. R. Forrester in *Christian Vocation:* "Contemplation to the Greeks and not merely to their philosophers is the highest kind of life, and leisure is nobler than work."

Similarly, high society of ancient Rome had its leisurely patrician class. It consisted not only of the "idle rich" who were self-indulging partygoers, sportsmen, and bathers but also of public-minded citizens intent on state service and the patronage of the arts. Typical of this group was Maecenas, a man of knightly status, wealth, high government career, and fondness for literature. He enabled the Roman poet Horace to devote himself to letters by presenting him with a country estate. But for that "Sabine farm," with the livelihood and leisure it afforded, some of Horace's odes might never have been written.

History shows that leisure for select minority groups, also in our land, is not new. What is different about America's burgeoning leisure at this time is its spread to the masses. Adding to the problem is the swiftness of leisure's advance, as David Riesman points out in *The Lonely Crowd:* "Because the distribution of leisure in America has been rapid as well as widespread, leisure presents Americans with issues that are historically new."

The massing of leisure for people not previously experiencing it may be illustrated by the figure of an inverted pyramid. In other times privileged persons crowding the point of the social pyramid — the noble, the idle elite, the lonely philosophers, the ruling group — had leisure, while the masses forming the base were chained to toil. In the upside-down world of today the masses fall heir to leisure, while executives of industry, college professors, doctors, lawyers, and other leaders in our society work the hardest. In geological terminology, a fault has occurred in our social structure. In the upheaval some strata are pushed up and others down. When there is a redistribution of wealth, the *nouveau riche* come into being. When there is a reapportionment of leisure, a corresponding new group emerges, with an abundance of free time in tenancy.

The leisure of our times is paradoxical in another

9

sense. People who are expected to have it in theory may not have it in practice. Consequently they may ask: "Where is all this leisure we are supposed to be enjoying? We are busier than ever!" Various explanations can be given for this anomaly. For one thing, a time lag is involved. It takes a while for the effects of leisure-producing movements to hit home uniformly to all individuals directly in the path of the storm. The full impact has not yet reached every potential candidate. Further, a person who by all logic should be in the eye of the hurricane may be on its periphery because he has taken a second job, works overtime, or is otherwise immersed in sideline activities. He is the exception rather than the rule.

Vignettes of Today's Leisure

What is the new leisure all about? What are examples of it? On the industrial scene it comes to dramatic focus in a Gary, Indiana, citizen and his wife who in midwinter said good-bye to friends and took a jet airliner to Florida for a three-month vacation with pay. The individual in question was not a man of wealth, not a bank president or semiretired chairman of the board. He was a steel worker beginning a 13-week "sabbatical" as provided for by contract between his labor union and the steel company. The "extended vacation" plan, pioneered by steel and can companies, is expected to spread to other industries. It means, in brief, that every fifth year workers under this plan will have more than a fourth of a year to themselves.

. . . Enoch W. Patten, a Chicago author and former newspaperman, writes: "I became a senior citizen at exactly 12:01 a. m. on my 65th birthday. Authorities tell me to cultivate a hobby, to collect things — stamps, butterflies, obsolete Mallet-type steam locomotives, anything that catches your fancy." Fortunately Patten has a better hobby. He is a man of letters and an authority on the writings of Charles Dickens. On retiring, so the Chicago *Tribune Magazine* reported, "he immediately took advantage of his new leisure to spend a month in England, comparing his impressions of the country with those of the master storyteller." This man is a member of a growing group, the retired, for whom leisure is either a pleasing or palling experience.

. . . The leisure here discussed is of domestic significance. It has the potential of revolutionizing not only the life of the wage earner but also that of the housewife. The whole kitchen economy of the modern home is geared to saving the homemaker's time and labor. It features deep-freeze units which keep fruits and vegetables fresh for table use. The kitchen chore of canning is eliminated. Many time-consuming culinary skills are now forgotten arts. Besides ready-mix ingredients we have ready-bake cakes, bread loaves, and rolls which need only be thrust into the oven for browning. In the home laundry department an entire Monday is no longer set aside for washday, for automatic washers and driers are within purchasing range of the average family. American industry offers housewives a plethora of time-saving, leisure-producing appliances and consumer goods.

. . . There is more leisure for children. Urban youngsters have practically no yardwork or household chores to do. There is no kindling or firewood to fetch, since the home is heated with gas, oil, or electricity. No milking has to be done; dairies deliver the milk to the house. Automatic dishwashers all but eliminate a daughter's task of helping with the dishes. Rural children of former years had miles to walk to school, and this took time. Nowadays most city children can walk to school in a matter of minutes. If the distance is considerable, as it is for some suburban children, mothers quite frequently take them and pick them up in the family station wagon.

. . . The age of leisure makes its impact on office workers, not only in that electronic computers eliminate many office jobs, but also in that people still doing office work enjoy "hidden leisure," or a more leisurely pace. The desk-fast clerical employee who knew an 8 a. m. to 6 p. m. schedule, Monday through Saturday, is gone. Ernest Havemann, in his *Life* magazine (Feb. 14, 1964) article, "The Emptiness of Too Much Leisure," gives a different, if slightly exaggerated, glimpse of today's office denizens:

> *"Consider a big-city office building, where the tenant firms stagger the workday hours to ease the pressure on commuting facilities and elevators. Anyone reporting at 9:30 a. m. is almost sure to have to fight his way into the lobby through a wave of 9 o'clock arrivers emerging for their first coffee break of the day. And anyone making a tour of the typical office at almost any hour is sure to see an extraordinary number of employees reading newspapers, working crossword puzzles, talking on the phone to friends, or giving themselves manicures."*

As these vignettes blend into a composite picture, we begin to see, in shadowy outlines at least, the extent of the new leisure movement. Shorter working hours, with more "coffee breaks" thrown in, are in store for industrial employees. At its 1964 convention, to show what is coming, the American Federation of Labor-Congress of Industrial Organizations pressed for a 35-hour week. A progressively diminishing work week, with a 30-hour week even now in prospect, is a near certainty. As working time in industry, homes, and business offices is cut down, leisure hours inevitably multiply like the proverbial family of rabbits.

12

The Meaning of Leisure

There are various ways to define leisure. The first meaning a dictionary gives for it connotes freedom from employment, occupation, or business. On this basis, leisure time stands for vocationally uncommitted hours, or the time a person has left over after performing his professional, income-producing work. It is evident, however, that people have other things to do besides working at their jobs. A second definition of leisure follows: freedom from any kind of obligatory engagement, or freedom synonymous with convenience and ease. Leisure time, by these terms, represents time remaining after the individual has discharged all job and *nonjob* duties devolving on him.

Let us make this distinction clear. A man performs income-producing work when for his and his family's livelihood he plows the north forty, sells brushes from door to door, or sets type in a newspaper plant. Each day he puts in a given number of hours in the exercise of his vocation. From the viewpoint of the job, the rest of the time is his own. As far as management is concerned, the employee is free to do with it as he pleases. The employer may even speak of it as the worker's free time.

From the worker's viewpoint, however, nonjob time may not be free time at all. The worker is responsible for other "must" activities. While off the job he must eat, sleep, shave, and the like. He spends several hours a week commuting. If he is a homeowner, he has to cut the lawn, paint the gutters, or trim the hedge. Of course, some men find it relaxing and pleasurable to do odd jobs at home and may not consider them work. The fact remains that these tasks have to be done, otherwise the property loses value and family life is adversely affected. It is only after the man has performed all duties incumbent

13

on him that he can be said to be at leisure, or have free time. It is along these lines that Charles K. Brightbill, in his *Man and Leisure, a Philosophy of Recreation,* explains leisure. Having enumerated the things a man must do: work at his job, sleep, rest, and attend to bodily needs, he goes on: "The time that remains is the *true* leisure, that period of time which becomes so significant to us to give serious thought to how it is used."

The word *leisure* (from the Latin *licere,* to be permitted) conveys the idea of permissiveness. In leisure a man is permitted to do what he likes, or leave it undone. He can pursue his hobby, chat with a neighbor across the back fence, read the newspaper, or refrain from all this and instead take a nap.

Leisure time, when compared with time spent on the job, seems considerable. It shrinks, however, when compared with time needed for both occupational and nonoccupational obligations. Sebastian de Grazia, a U. S. political scientist and author of the Twentieth Century Fund-financed study, *Of Time, Work and Leisure,* takes the position that free time is not as abundant as often claimed. He has computed that the average male worker is on the job 47 hours a week, spends 8½ hours traveling to and from his job, and is occupied for 7 more hours doing odd jobs at home. This totals to 62½ hours a week, roughly corresponding with the time that workmen of previous generations devoted to jobs. The point de Grazia wants to make is this: When it comes to the actual enjoyment of leisure time, the modern worker is not much better off than his predecessors.

The definitions cited earlier point to leisure as *freedom* from or for something. They reflect a conception of leisure which relates to a state of mind rather than the clock. Leisure as a mood and leisure as free time are not the same according to this distinction. Writes Josef Pieper: "Leisure, it must be clearly understood, is a mental

14

and spiritual attitude — it is not simply the result of external factors, it is not the inevitable result of spare time, a holiday, a weekend, or a vacation. It is, in the first place, an attitude of mind, a condition of the soul."

Sebastian de Grazia, like Pieper of a philosophic frame of mind, is also among those who insist that leisure should be distinguished from free time, or from what is commonly called leisure time, because he feels it is a thing of the mind rather than a matter of hours. He writes in the mentioned study: "Work is the antonym of free time. But not of leisure. . . . Free time refers to a special way of calculating a special kind of time. Leisure refers to a state of being, a condition of man, which few desire and fewer achieve."

The above distinction has value, not so much because it attempts to differentiate between free time and leisure — for most people this is a distinction without a difference — but because it shows that it is largely up to the person himself to turn free time, which can be barren and boring, into fruitful time. For our purposes it is not necessary to draw a sharp line between leisure, leisure time, and free time. We are concerned in this presentation about leisure in the sense of uncommitted hours — the time people have on their hands after discharging both their job and non-job obligations. These uncommitted hours we shall interchangeably refer to as leisure, leisure time, or free time.

Causes of the New Leisure

Usually the growth of leisure is laid at the door of automation. That automation is throwing people out of work, at least temporarily, cannot be questioned. The U. S. Secretary of Labor has estimated that automation dries up 2 million jobs a year. In not every instance are workers outrightly dismissed. They may be displaced indirectly, or in "silent firings." It means: because jobs are wiped out, new workers are not hired.

How the new process of cybernetics eliminates jobs is illustrated from business and service industries close to everyone's home. The telephone system and banks used to absorb many young women in the 18—24 age bracket for jobs as operators and machine bookkeepers respectively. Both industries, converting to automation over a short span of years, are hiring less personnel for this work. Between 1950 and 1960 the number of telephone operators dropped from 130,000 to 81,000. All the while 31 million telephones were in use — an all-time high. As the volume of traffic increased 80 percent, 40 percent fewer operators were hired. The ratio becomes more disparate as time goes on. In former years two typical New York City banks customarily hired some 150 machine bookkeepers a year. When in 1963 they introduced the Magnetic Ink Character Recognition system — an automation code featuring those strange numbers and symbols appearing on checks — not a single machine bookkeeper was engaged.

It is difficult to predict how public service, business housekeeping, and industrial production by electronic "brains" will ultimately affect the employment picture. To some extent, automation also creates jobs by opening up new areas of enterprise. Because machines are replacing men as workers, counters, and "thinkers," many people will be caught in the middle. They will have to make the transition from one type of employment to another. During the change-over there will be periods of unemployment and enforced leisure. Automation is closely tied to the leisure question. It is sure to replace workers and shorten working hours because of its tremendous ability to turn out goods in minimum time. And this means more leisure.

Aside from automation, other causes of leisure must

be cited. They include the comparative affluence of our society, great productive capacity, population growth, improved transportation and communication, and early retirement. Not to be overlooked is the lengthening of the average person's life span. The longer a person lives in his retired or semiretired state, the longer is also his leisure time. People who retire sooner and live longer form an expanding leisure group as an important segment of our society. The 3 million men holding second jobs and the 17 million women in full-time employment also have an effect on the leisure movement. The father in "moonlighting" and the mother in "sunlighting" increase the family income for use in leisure-time activities.

Effects of the New Leisure

Leisure not only results from something; it is also the cause of, or incentive to, far-reaching changes in American life. It opens new avenues of activities. It gives impetus to new industries manufacturing equipment for leisure-time pursuits. People enjoying more leisure and having paychecks to match create demands for new things. The big change from the past is that leisure becomes "consumptive time," that is, people have turned from producers in labor to consumers in leisure. The effect is a new mass market for goods and services which in the past were restricted to people of special privilege.

The economic aspect of the new leisure era is considerable, for free time is connected with prosperity, or, as Brightbill puts it: leisure has a "link with legal tender." The cost of free-time activities in the United States falls somewhere between 20 and 40 billion dollars a year, depending on what is included under amusement or recreation expenses. It costs from $2,736 to $5,486 to build a private swimming pool. Houseboats, in which many leisure hours are spent, cost approximately $6,000. "There is no question that the houseboat is about to become the new bonanza in the boating field," writes Eric Nyborg, boating editor of *Argosy* magazine. Other types of leisure activity are likewise costly. One hobby alone, namely remote-controlled miniature sport-car racing, a pastime kindred to the miniature electric train hobby, is in the $25 million-a-year class.

The new leisure is unique because it affects our economy from another point of view: it is connected with nonwork income, or the possibility of having a workless livelihood. Sylvia Porter, a syndicated newspaper commentator on financial and economic affairs, calls this way of life "the occupation of nonwork." It means: Not the individual, but his money is working and earning. The occupation of nonwork, says this writer, "ranks unchallenged at the top of the fastest-growing sources of personal income." In one year 7,300,000 Americans drew an income of $100 billion from dividends, interest, rent, Social Security benefits, and other sources. Probably the greatest nonwork source of income for ex-workers is Social Security, whose payments since 1952 have increased 550 percent. The occupation of nonwork, or the leisure way of life, contributes heavily to what Robert M. Hutchins labels "our workless world."

Increasing leisure has not only economic but also social consequences. Social scientists stress that our culture, largely under the impact of leisure, is shifting its weight to new foundations. The style of living, sociologically speaking, is basically different when people spend less time at their jobs and far more time in leisure occupations. Undergirding the new mode of life is a changed social philosophy. In the transference of social values, the prestige, priority, and sovereignty which in past years people associated with their jobs is now frequently given over to leisure-time enterprises.

In 1860 the average worker spent 68.0 hours at his

job. If computed on the basis of a five-day week, he was putting in 13.6 hours a day. Such long hours well-nigh dictated the kind of social life possible, or impossible, for men and their families. A man's job was sovereign; everything else was subsidiary to it. What free time there was, mostly on Sunday afternoons, had to be utilized for rest. It is evident: a man under these circumstances would be too exhausted to step out with his wife socially on an evening, engage in do-it-yourself projects at home, or participate in community affairs, such as Little League or Cub Scouts.

In 1960 the hours per week on the job had shrunk to 37.5, while the working day had diminished to 7.5 hours. This means: the average working man of today has much more free time, and this fact influences the kind of life he leads in society.

The effects of leisure penetrate to the cultural dimension. The American people of the past had a record as go-getters, activists, and pragmatists with respect to their work. They were then not inclined to visit art museums, attend concerts, make beaten paths to public libraries, or listen to "uplift" lectures. A change of habits is in the making, with leisure playing a major role as a contributing factor. An indication of greater cultural appreciation is the fact that 14 million Americans now attend concerts every year. There is manifest interest in the "little theater" movement. When the Mona Lisa painting was shown in various cities, people stood in line for hours to view it.

Our still incipient age of leisure makes a telling mark on the mood of individuals in yet another way. As one would expect, it has a psychological effect. Popular reaction to leisure is not uniformly the same. While many welcome more free time and seemingly thrive under it, others wilt under it because they are emotionally unprepared for it.

A part of the problem is that Americans, because of

previous training and conditioning, are apt to transfer work habits to leisure time. They are unhappy unless they can see something practical in free-time activities and can clothe them with a sense of purpose. If they go out golfing on a day off, they find it hard to enjoy the game, the sunshine, and fresh air. Something tells them they must perfect their drives and putts; that time is wasted unless they do a good job at playing golf; that the game justifies itself if it opens doors to new friendships or new business contacts. Perhaps even a practical idea or an inspiration for the solution of a problem will flash into the mind on the greens.

Since leisure does not lend itself to pragmatic patterns, it tends to be a wounding experience for some. During free time the bottom seems to drop out of things. Psychiatrists speak of people who come to them with an emotional disease called "weekend neurosis." These patients are so accustomed to the Monday-through-Friday work schedule that, with this framework removed, they go to pieces during the Saturday-Sunday interlude.

Challenge of the Leisure Age

The multiplication of leisure for the broad populace raises a host of problems. National leaders and the people themselves will grapple with them for years to come. Automation, with leisure as a by-product, is certain to mark the end of an era. Yesterday's adage of father laboring from sun to sun while mother's work is never done, as far as the average American in an urban setting is concerned, is more descriptive of the past than the present. Leisure comes over the horizon as either a helpful friend or a haunting specter. It can be a benefactor to mankind. It can also be a tyrannical, oppressive, and long-staying visitor wearing out its welcome, like the importune guest in the play *The Man Who Came to Dinner*.

Pressing questions attend the development of a leisure-laden way of life. If it is true, as a knowledgeable writer claims, that "each of us has at our daily disposal as much power — as many services — as would in pre-industrial days have required 90 slaves," the question certainly arises: What will people do with leisure without themselves becoming slaves to boredom and victims of machines affording them relief from time-consuming toil? If automation will enable a small portion of our population to do all the work for a nation, what will the majority do? Can management absorb displaced workers? How many can enter service professions? Aside from "selling each other second mortgages," as a young Los Angeles executive put it, what will people do to make a living? What will they do with leisure?

Coming closer to existing leisure problems, what will a Gary, Ind., steel worker do with his 13-week "sabbatical" if he lacks funds and the mental capacity to use the time for travel and cultural self-improvement? How can the Akron, Ohio, factory employees working a 36-hour week spend their free time to good advantage? What, besides overtime pay, does the 25-hour base week, with its accompanying leisure, mean to electrical construction workers now in New York City? What does the age of leisure hold in store for insufficiently educated people — for the 7.5 million young people who annually drop out of high school? How welcome are "honeydew days" ("Honey, do this, do that!") to men who spend entire weekdays at home and run errands for their wives? On the distaff side, do women appreciate having grumbling husbands under their feet in daytime? Does more leisure occasion tensions in marriage and other life situations?

Year by year the list of such questions will grow. It is time to assess the assets and liabilities of leisure and to begin balancing the books.

2

USES OF
THE NEW LEISURE

What are Americans doing with the largess of new leisure?
What they do depends considerably on personal circumstances, preferences, age, sex, interests, degree of cultural
development, geographical localities, and other variables.
In general, proliferating free time prompts notable up-
swings in a wide variety of self-expressive, pleasurable,
and change-of-pace activities. In some instances new
leisure enterprises are highly commercialized; in others,
cost is not a factor. The forms of pastimes chosen run
the gamut of human amusements, from restful indoor
diversions to highly active outdoor sports, from complete
disengagement to demanding involvement. The pursuits
reflect individualism as well as group conformity.

Television Viewing

To be sure, more people are watching television programs. The TV set is a typical leisure-age symbol. It requires passivity on the part of the viewer. People can listen to radio while working or driving their cars. Television is different in that it enlists both the eye and the ear, virtually compelling the person to be totally at rest while receiving its message.

The U. S. Census Bureau estimates that, as of January 1962, over 56 million television sets were in use in American homes. In September 1963, according to a C. A. Nielsen Company count, 92 percent of United States homes were supplied with at least one set. The increase of time spent before TV screens is noted. During January and February of 1963 the average American family gave six hours and eight minutes a day to television viewing. This was an increase of ten minutes a day over the time so spent in the corresponding period in 1962. As one would expect, most people were found watching TV at night. At that, afternoon viewing claimed more than a third of the total hours devoted to television. Supplying the programs were 657 stations in the United States and about 70 in Canada.

More Reading

People of leisure are spending more time reading books and magazines. In doing so they become a market for the products of the printing press, notably for paperbacks now flooding the book world. Between 300 and 400 softcover books are added every month to the more than 25 thousand titles already in print. According to the American Book Publishing Council, the publication of all kinds of books went up 445 per cent between 1940 and 1960. In the periodicals field it is noteworthy that a magazine entitled *Leisure* has, since January 1960, taken its place on newsstands, along with *Time, Life, Holiday, Camping News, Sporting News,* and the like. Some magazines have special editors for such leisure-time activities as boating.

Sports and Recreation

The pleasure-boat business has been booming in recent years. Sunday editions of metropolitan newspapers carry advertisements of new and used boats, as they do of automobiles. The Boat Show is one of the gala events coming annually to Chicago's convention and exhibit center, McCormick Place. *Life* magazine, in a special leisure edition, referred to the boat trend as reflecting a "national aquamania." It reported that 8 million recreational boats were plying our waters.

The new, largely leisure-born interest in water sports expresses itself in other forms: swimming, surfboard riding, water skiing, and scuba diving. From water sports stem special hobbies, some "in" and some "out," as interests change. From spearfishing some divers have advanced to underwater pursuits more challenging to their skills, such as hunting for sunken treasures. For weekend sailors pushbutton gearshifting for outboard motors was "in." For people staying at home, private swimming pools — they jumped from 2,500 in 1948 to 250,000 in 1962 — in backyards and water-sport facilities in home communities are popular.

The new leisure invites to participation in other recreational pastimes. The 1963 *Britannica Book of the Year* reports: "Americans were spending more time and money on leisure pleasures, both indoor and out, than ever before. In 1962, 32,000,000 Americans were bowling, and the figure was increased by 1,000,000 a year.

From other sources of information come much the

same data. More Americans were participating in such forms of amusement and recreation as card playing, chess, strategy games, and, especially the young, in science experiments. Do-it-yourself diversion at home and in public showed greater increase than did attendance at spectator sports. Interest in athletic contests is shifting, with the fans showing preference for the spectacular. Major league baseball is fading as "the national pastime." More spectators are crowding professional football stadia and the arenas of other, more pronounced action sports, such as hockey and stock-car racing.

Reuel Denney asks in his book, *The Astonished Muse:* "What do people do when they are not satisfied with the movies and TV, and when they react against merely spectatorial relationships to the world of sports?" He replies: "They make things, or they participate in some sort of performance or contest themselves."

Americans show themselves "joiners" in leisure enterprises. It is not enough to work at hobbies at home. The next step is to join clubs organized around such hobbies. The result is the formation of more bridge clubs, garden clubs, and antique car clubs. The clubs afford more than inspiration and hints for the perfection of one's hobby. Along with the exchange of ideas goes fellowship. Like the guilds of old, the clubs help meet the social needs of members. With people becoming more isolated in the break-up of traditional community life, it is no surprise that they seek self-identity and sociability in leisure-time clubs.

Prospering are not only hobby shops selling coins, stamps, or rare books, but also business firms catering to assorted leisure-time interests. Pet shops are among the latter. As a rule, pet-animal stores are found in such parts of the city and its suburbs where children abound. However, also adults buy tropical fish, canary birds, puppies, and whatever else the modern "Noah's ark" of a pet shop stocks. Many lonesome grownups find companion-ship in animals. Men and women in the stream of life are leisure-time fanciers of particular breeds of dogs and cats. The popular dog and cat shows held in sophisticated cities and drawing entries from all over the country attest to the widespread leisure-time preoccupation with animals.

While conformism is much in evidence in free-time recreation, it is also true that some disregard fads and go their individual ways to find diversion. Ex-President Truman takes brisk morning walks. Ex-President Eisen-hower is a devotee to the golf game. The Kennedy family is fond of touch football. Dr. Paul Dudley White, the famous heart surgeon, gets his exercise and fresh air bicycling. The present age provides many options for the kind of recreation the individual prefers. In leisure, David Riesman points out, "there is still room left for the would-be autonomous man to reclaim his individual char-acter from the pervasive demands of his social character." In other words, the person can do as he likes.

Other Activities

In the new-leisure situation people do other things to engage their minds and emotions. Churchill, Eisenhower, and other prominent figures find relaxation in painting pictures. Following their example are 10 million American amateur painters. Their works may never grace the walls of the Louvre in Paris or the Metropolitan Museum of Art in New York. Perhaps the best one could expect is their entry in local art fairs. Better still, "art for art's sake" applies here. The individual paints for his own pleasure, satisfied that he is expressing his artistic feeling and talent in the best way he can. In another art area, 11 million Americans are amateur musicians.

Adult-education classes annually absorb 13 million

Americans. Education offers one of the main outlets for the purposeful use of leisure. To the advantage of people desiring to continue learning in fields of special interest, many high schools and neighborhood colleges list evening or extension courses for adults. The opportunity is afforded to acquire professional and pastime skills. A high school in suburban Chicago listed evening courses in knitting, millinery, personal typing, intermediate typing, electronic data processing, and principles and practices of real estate. There is an element of discipline or regimen in taking organized courses and doing the required home reading. However, many Americans are furthering knowledge also under more informal conditions as they engage in private reading and other mind-stretching exercises without benefit of courses.

Granted more free time and better incomes, Americans are travelers. Tourism, both abroad and at home, is big business. Travel abroad, since World War II, increased in volume sixfold. Americans on the move frequent vacationlands in continental United States. Luxury motels, supplied with TV, air conditioning, and swimming pools, dot the country wherever the concrete ribbons of highways run their course. In more recent years a reaction has set in to expensive lodging. Not all tourists want the comfort of home when on the road. The trend now, especially for family travel, is to camp out under more primitive conditions. The attractive feature of this touring style is the change of pace it affords from family living at home. Children accustomed to urban life have the opportunity to discover the great outdoors.

Home Life and Leisure

The home has become a greater focal point for leisure-time activities. At home the individual can be more of a complete person. For many workers the job no longer satisfies the human craving for wholeness. This is particularly true of assembly-line workers, both men and women, who perform only a fractional part in the manufacture of total products. Work under these conditions is for many a "necessary evil" to be endured only for the sake of paychecks and their "open sesame" to life's more interesting things. Work is something to get away from as soon as possible to be at liberty to do what one likes. Gone is the sense of satisfaction which in former years skilled craftsmen found in the perfection of whole products.

With less time spent at work (and less inclination to spend it there), where does the worker find satisfaction? Speaking of the shift of interest, Margaret Mead states: "The generation which has married since the war has responded to these conditions by shifting the balance from work . . . to the home. The home in which one was once allowed a limited amount of recuperation and recreation in reward for working hard, has now become the reason for existence which in turn justifies working at all. . . . Hours of work which permit a man to spend more time at home, length of vacation, amount of strain and over-work, all are valued as to how they affect family life. As once it was wrong to play so hard that it might affect one's work, now it is wrong to work so hard that it may affect family life."

What are people, particularly the heads of families, doing with their home leisure? The do-it-yourself movement for home owners continues, not only because tradesmen — carpenters, plumbers, interior decorators — charge highly for their work but also because the man of the house is himself looking for something to do. He finds an outlet for his creative skills by building things the family can use. His projects may be putting pine boards on basement walls, assembling a stereo set, or increasing shelf space in the kitchen. The typical suburban home with its surrounding yard presents the resident with many challenges for evening and weekend work.

The housewife and mother, perhaps less aware of the new leisure tide than other members of society, has more free moments for things she likes to do. The telephone is hers for chats with friends. In midforenoon neighbors drop in for coffee breaks and tension-relieving conversation. Community organizations — Parent-Teacher Association, mothers' clubs for youth groups — lay claim to the homemaker's free time. Electronic and mechanical "maids" in kitchen, laundryroom, and the house as a whole enable the American homemaker to participate in more leisure pursuits.

The Nonuse of Leisure

Pascal has written: "All the unhappiness of men arises from one single fact, that they cannot stay quietly in their own chamber." This observation describes many Americans. Schooled in activism and now smothered with leisure, they are at a loss to know what to do — what to do with themselves. People entering early retirement are among the worst victims of "barren boredom" for want of non-work interests. Havemann, in the *Life* article cited earlier, writes: "One university study of retired steelworkers, for example, showed that most of them joyously spent the first year doing all the fishing they had dreamed of. Three years later most of these same men did not even own a fishing rod and, as a matter of fact, did nothing much but sit around, silent and glum, presumably wishing they were young enough to go back to a job."

For people who can "stay quietly in their own chamber" there is recreative value in do-nothing leisure. For those lacking this aptitude, free time can be most boring. By the irony of fate the "wrong" people are frequently in possession of leisure. These are persons who by intelligence-test scores are shown to be incapable of formal education, and oldsters too far along in life to be retreaded for the leisure demands of the new age. For them free time represents a blank. The vernacular saying: "Nothing to do, and all day to do it in" describes their situation. In view of facts like these, Arthur Schlesinger, Jr., has said: "The most dangerous threat hanging over American society is the threat of leisure." He added: "Those who have the least preparation for leisure will have the most of it."

The Abuse of Leisure

Experts examining uses of the new leisure for fishing, television, and spectator sports are not agreed that this is good. Some say: Americans should be guided to more satisfying activities. They are answered by members of the *laissez-faire* school who say: Let the American people alone, to do with free time as they like. Must they always be supervised? A third group deplores the abuse of leisure resulting in the waste of human talents and potentialities and in moral deterioration.

In *Life Looks Up* Charles B. Templeton touches on the influence of people in our lives. He goes on: "There is another kind of bad company: the things that are our daily companions, the books we read, the magazines we devour, the television and radio programs to which we are addicted, the thoughts and ideas that dominate our mind. Who can doubt but what our lives are profoundly influenced by these daily companions of our leisure hours?"

The abuse of leisure gives us pause to reflect. Moralists, however secular their orientation, face the problem of the questionable use of free time and its downright misuse. Given persons demoralized by purposeless leisure and lacking moral character, the temptation is great to drift into an assortment of activities commonly recognized as vices. The temptation is heightened when a lot of loose money is floating around for the cultivation of undesirable habits.

Drinking and Gambling

More free time can aid and abet the consumption of alcohol beyond the limits of safety and health. In the fall of 1963 the Distilled Spirits Institute of Washington, D. C., released a statistical report on the use of liquor for a twelve-month period. It cited 257,044,292 as the number of gallons of liquor drunk by Americans in one year. To show that our economy is expanding also in the alcoholic front, the Institute claimed a 4.5 percent increase over the previous year. It is worth someone's time to investigate in a depth study whether there is a relation between greater alcohol consumption and the disease of alcoholism, and whether one or the other, or both, should be considered in connection with leisure. Is it possible that many resort to drink because excessive free time is turning sour and causing boredom?

It is an open secret that many workingmen with less to do spend more time in neighborhood taverns. Wives interviewed in a nationwide Gallup poll in 1957 mentioned drinking by their husbands as one of their reasons for opposing a four-day work week. Harvey Swados, in *Mass Leisure,* phrased their opposition thus: "There is the fear that the husband who is off for three days may become less responsible, drink more, run around more."

A twin evil apt to thrive with the multiplication of uncommitted leisure hours is gambling. Local "horse parlors" and other betting establishments are doing well — too well, in fact. Max Kaplan reports: "The Kefauver Crime Committee's estimate that *illegal* gambling of all kinds totaled 20 billion dollars a year, or twice the gross

turnover of the automobile industry, the country's largest."
What harmful effects does gambling have? What is apt
to happen when 17 million Americans regularly play
bingo? The questions have a distinct moral aspect, of
course. Speaking from a purely social standpoint, gambling
has these results, according to Kaplan: "Other leisure
activities, such as gambling away resources needed for
one's family, have objective consequences harmful by
standards of indebtedness, mental health, or family solidarity."

Loafing and High Living

Many misuses of leisure carry over from previous eras,
representing what people have always done to express
inordinate passions, drives, and impulses. The new leisure
comes into consideration here only because it provides
more opportunities to multiply or intensify the action.
From time immemorial, misdeeds have marred the use
of free time, especially in places where people congregate
in community life. No town is so small but that it may
harbor habitual loafers, poolhall characters, and men who
sit idly in front of stores, ogling women, telling dirty jokes,
and punctuating conversations with volleys of profanity.
The big city has its facilities for degrading amusements,
among them certain night clubs and "key clubs," honky-
tonks, dens of iniquity, and the inevitable houses of ill
fame. Tired businessmen, local playboys, visiting firemen,
out-of-town conventioners, and those celebrating special
events, like on New Year's Eve, are notable examples
of people abusing leisure in the city's gay spots.

Some abuses of leisure escape public censure, not because they are morally better than the more exhibitionistic
instances just recited, but because they are practiced in
private or with an aura of greater respectability. The
town gossips sipping tea behind lace curtains and cutting

their victims to pieces with slandering tongue are no less mismanaging leisure hours than are individuals out painting the town red. Idleness — the misuse of leisure — is the devil's workshop in many ways. The idle tongue is by no means an exception to such abuse.

Going into Debt

Americans are prone to buy merchandise "on time," both things they need and things they don't need. The pleasures of leisure are also available on an "enjoy now — pay later" basis. Vacation trips can be taken on credit cards. Recreational equipment can be purchased on the installment plan. Ordinarily there is nothing amiss or indiscreet about that, provided that payments can be made as per schedule.

For some the lure of leisure and of leisure gear leads to an overstrain on the family budget, with the result that necessities have to be sacrificed in favor of luxury items. For lack of payment, repossession proceedings may be initiated. The buyer loses his equity or may go deeper into debt because the original loan has to be refinanced. Some families have to face the fact that they simply cannot afford the prestige symbols of a leisure society: sport cars, luxury boats, private swimming pools, trips to Nassau, and whatever else. Leisure time spent in too grand a style entails penalties instead of real pleasures.

The abuse of leisure in social status building or in the aforementioned vices reveals a moral gap in individuals and in American society as a whole. Leisure activities become showcases exhibiting people at their true, uninhibited selves, with the specimens displayed frequently leaving much to be desired. Kaplan writes: "Leisure deals with hours and ways of behavior in which we are freest to be ourselves. Thus what we do, whether on the noblest of levels and aspirations or the lowest of tastes, is a clue or indication of *what* we are, *who* we are, *where* we want to go. The morality of our entertainment — quiz shows on television or illegal gambling on school sports — cannot be separated from the morality of our whole life. In our leisure we stand exposed. Through our leisure we provide the elements for diagnosing our culture to the observer."

Retreat into Privatism

The release of people from the tyranny of jobs for more time to be spent at home can be to the good of the family. The retreat to home life entails also a liability if it represents flight from the responsibilities of larger community life. Home projects can become blotters absorbing all the individual's interests and abstracting them from the public good. The early-marriage trend is a symptom of youth's retreat into privatism. In an interview published in *U. S. News & World Report*, Margaret Mead said:

> *Nobody is going to be interested in doing anything except having children. And you can't run a society if everybody's main interest in life is domestic — if nobody wants to be a Senator or a Governor or a President; if nobody wants to be inventor, the lonely thinker. The average American today is more interested in being a father than he is in his career job.*

> *Most of our young professional people these days have several children before they ever get their final degree. Twenty years ago, law students talked to other law students about the law. Medical students talked to other medical students about medicine. Theological students talked about theology. Now these students are home giving the baby its bottle, or helping with the housework.*

In brief, the man of former years who was on the job 60 to 70 hours a week had too little time for his family. The man of today, under the avalanche of new leisure, is apt to be home too much. He is tempted to bury himself too deeply in home and family affairs. Both extremes — too much time on the job, too much leisure at home — involve the same hazard: too little time, too little energy, too little interest remain for participation in public affairs.

The uses, nonuses, and abuses of the new leisure reveal a situation far from uniformally healthy for persons and the nation as such. Details in the composite picture show leisure practices which are sound, leisure potentialities whose surfaces are barely scratched, and leisure perils. The question before the collective house of the American people on the eve of the automation revolution is this: How can we make optimum use of our newfound leisure? It is a question to which people themselves, under the guidance of competent leaders, must give answer.

3

APPROACHES
TO THE NEW LEISURE

The new leisure enters sufficiently into the domain of public welfare as to engage the attention of national leaders in many fields. Representative observers advocate many kinds of approaches to its opportunities and problems. Their suggestions range from information programs to measures growing out of present operations for the public good to special crash projects dealing entirely with leisure.

More specifically, the method of dealing with the situation, as various spokesmen define it, has three aspects. The first phase is the creation of awareness — sometimes by overstatement — that mass leisure is here. This is more than "just talk." It presupposes that informed persons can on their own initiative devise ways and means to cope with leisure affecting them. The second phase, which is already a step toward solution by corporate action, con-

36

sists in relating leisure to various enterprises now in effect. It suggests, for example, the absorption of leisure into adult education movements already in full career. It may also see at least a partial solution to free-time problems in the achievement of full employment, for which official machinery exists. This approach considers the answer to leisure as contingent on finding answers to other, more pressing problems. The third phase, predicated on the assumption that excessive free time is a national crisis, looks to a direct, all-out assault on leisure. One or more of these steps will become evident as we briefly survey expressions of concern on the subject.

Organized Labor and Leisure

The education division of the American Federation of Labor-Congress for Industrial Organizations, as early as 1959, sponsored a conference in Washington, D. C., on the theme "Education for Retirement and Leisure." The conference came to grips with obvious developments in the labor field: the gradual takeover of jobs by automation, the shorter work week, early retirement made possible by pensions and Social Security payments, and the purposeful redemption of leisure accruing to pensioners and payrollers. Education was heavily stressed as one of the prime means for turning free time to good use.

The leadership of organized labor finds itself in a peculiar dilemma. On the one hand, to spread work to as many people as possible, it urges a shorter work week. On the other, it feels called on to advise its members on what to do with the resultant leisure. In evidence is a sense of social responsibility and a humane concern for people. The fact is recognized that more leisure is not automatically wholesome for workers. This explains the effort of labor headquarters to offer guidance on its prudential use.

The Voice of Government

Making itself a party to the American public's experience of more leisure is the government, both state and national. Official concern is voiced on many counts, in the main on leisure-related problems affecting the aged, the retired, the chronically unemployed, the disabled, poverty-stricken people, migratory workers, young people unable to find work, and also women. In various contexts the leisure question emerges as pertinent to the national welfare.

While touring the Western states in the fall of 1963 the late President John F. Kennedy connected leisure problems with the preservation and development of the country's natural resources. Referring to the use of public lands, particularly national parks for leisure-time recreation, the President said, "As machines take more and more of the jobs of men, we are going to find the work week reduced, and we are going to find people wondering what they should do." He envisioned the possibility of future citizens facing the dilemma of having free time for recreation but no places where to spend it. President Kennedy, on this occasion, showed the vision of a true statesman. He foresaw the interrelationship of developing problems. When there is a disproportionate relation between free time and free space, life — and with it national morale — gets out of balance for masses confined to cramped living quarters in the cities.

The leisure factor is implicit in many operational and projected programs aimed at human conservation. The husbanding of the talents of young people bulks large in these concerns. The government is aware not only of the 7.5 million youths who are high school dropouts and post-high school fizz-outs but also of the more talented (but insufficiently trained) teen-agers facing the automation age. As the government sees it, it is a waste of human resources to consign able and willing young people to a life of sterile leisure. The success of the Peace Corps, as one way of enlisting the services of youth and keeping world peace from becoming a corpse, assures the launching of other programs for youth.

Human conservation and development are key concepts in the report of the President's Commission on the Status of Women, a 22-month study published in the fall of 1963. Among its many recommendations for the better utilization of womanpower the Commission called for "a more rewarding use of leisure time" and for "interesting and constructive use of a woman's time and talents during the 30 years she is likely to live after age 40."

Education for the Leisure Age

"In the new age of science and space, improved education is essential to give new meaning to our national purpose and power," said John F. Kennedy in his presidential message on education delivered to the Congress, January 29, 1963. The word "leisure" is not expressly mentioned in the address. It is evident, however, that the role of education in the age of space studies, science, technology, and automation applies per-force to leisure. These are further highlights from the President's message:

For the individual, the doors of the schoolhouse, to the library, and to the college lead to the richest treasures of our open society: to the power of knowledge — to the training and skills necessary for productive employment — to the wisdom, the ideals, and the culture which enrich life — and to the creative, self-disciplined understanding of society needed for good citizenship in today's changing and challenging world.

Nearly 40 percent of our youths are dropping out before graduating from high school; only 43 percent of our adults have completed high school; only 8 percent

39

of our adults have complete college; and only 16 per-cent of our young people are presently completing college.

The percentages quoted applied to the situation then prevailing. That a definite turning point had been reached in favor of more education is evident from a later passage in the address. In taking account of changes for the immediate present, and in projecting a new type of education for the future, the speaker said in other climactic statements:

Nearly 50 million people were enrolled in our schools and colleges in 1962 — an increase of more than 50 percent since 1950. By 1970, college enrollment will be nearly double, and secondary schools will increase enrollment by 50 percent.

We need an appraisal of the entire range of educational problems, viewing educational opportunity as a continuous, lifelong process, starting with preschool training and extending through elementary and secondary schools, college, graduate education, vocational training, job training and retraining, adult education, and such general community educational resources as the public library.

These excerpts are relevant to the leisure condition, and that from several points of view. For one thing, lack of education often leads to unemployment, or a state of involuntary leisure. A bulletin of the U. S. Office of Education states: "We have long known that unemployment is closely related to levels of education." How close that relation is was established by research work done at Virginia State College. According to the bulletin, the findings show that "one out of every ten workers who failed to finish elementary school is unemployed today, as compared to one out of 50 college graduates."

Apart from the employment situation, a further point

40

concerns the new quality of education needed to prepare for life in a leisure-filled society. The President spoke clearly on this issue when he referred to "the wisdom, the ideals, and the culture which enrich life" and subsequently to "the creative, self-disciplined understanding of society." From now on, he advocated, let education be a "life-long process," and let there be emphasis on "adult education" and on "such general community educational resources as the public library." These are seminal statements indicating ideas to be developed for the more fruitful use of time and talents in the age of leisure.

Other qualified observers envision more education — not more golf, more hobbies, more fishing, more TV-viewing — as offering a satisfactory solution to leisure-time problems. Milton R. Stern, assistant dean of New York University, has publicly stated that more adult education for everybody is not only desirable but "may soon become compulsory." Sylvia Porter, in a series of syndicated newspaper columns on leisure, approved Dr. Stern's suggestions and added: "The answer (to extended leisure time) is a step-up in education of the American adult, as well as the young, to prepare all of us to reach a higher plateau of literacy in every sphere — economic, political, social, cultural."

For a leisure society come of age, the new quality of education suggests an approach differing from the "get ahead" philosophy still undergirding much of the public school curriculum. The "get ahead" emphasis, so deeply engrained in the American character, harks back to a time when education was regarded a tool for rugged individualism, for self-advancement. And self-advancement meant mostly the acquisition of material goods. In an age when automation and leisure come to maturity, material things, which are within everyone's reach, are no longer status symbols. Gleaming automobiles, homes on a suburban spread, furs and jewelry for the wife — people in America's broad middle class can afford them now. Prestige values shift now to performances of excellence, personal creativity, cultural appreciation, and services through one's realized talent potentialities. Public school education, so say our social scientists, ought to adjust itself to the spirit of the new leisure age.

Increasingly desirable and necessary for school children in the leisure era is grounding in an area of studies known as the humanities. The reason for educating people in "the wisdom, the ideals, and the culture which enrich life" are at least twofold: (1) to counterbalance the heavy demands of vocational specialization which our technological society makes on people, and (2) to impart competence for the enriching use of leisure during nonworking hours. Interest in the humanities — literature, poetry, language studies, history, the arts — will, in the first instance, keep people from being mechanical robots in our button-pushing dial-watching, computer-controlled style of industrial production and, in the second instance, keep them from being cultural morons during free time. A broad education will be needed to give an overall view of life, in contrast to the narrow "tunnel vision" of technological specialists.

The reverse side of the coin shows that everyone's education in the future will contain more mathematics and science. On an exchange basis, engineers will study social sciences, ethics, languages, aesthetics; and nonengineers will return the compliment by studying mathematics, physics, chemistry. The outcome of this "two-way stretch" of education is that two types of people can again converse intelligently and unite their mental resources for the good of the community. In addition, a better climate is created for both groups for the enjoyment of leisure. There is value for a technologist to read poetry and Shakespearian drama during free hours, and there is profit for a high school French instructor, for example, to develop hobby interests in science.

The Business Community and Leisure

The business world has a vital stake in the progress of the leisure movement. Its interest extends beyond manufacturing and marketing goods for use in free time. Socially-minded leaders in commercial fields, from Main Street in Hometown, U. S. A., to Wall Street in New York City, realize that factors other than profit and purchasing power are involved in the leisure phenomenon. Beyond consumer goods indices, the dollar sign, and Gross National Product figures are human values. People need more than material things if they are to meet the challenge of the leisure age.

As automation ushers more workers out of jobs and forces on them an uncertain future, business management is becoming increasingly aware of its responsibility to mobilize its resources for the public welfare. It makes its contribution, in terms of counsel as well as cash, when it participates with other leaders in society in preparing displaced jobholders for other modes of livelihood, grants subsidies to vocational schools and colleges, makes scholarships available, and issues educational reading matter bearing on leisure-related problems.

Life and health insurance companies are "big business" these days. Few commercial firms are in so favorable a position to coordinate enlightened self-interests with the well-being of the people. A sizable leisure group in our population depends on life insurance dividends and other earnings for supplementary income. Giant corporations, and that is what many old-line life insurance companies are, reveal their souls in the measure that they serve the people's interests.

By way of illustration, the New York Life Insurance Company, through its Career Information Services, makes free booklets available on nearly every conceivable vocation or profession. Some of the booklet titles are: *Should*

You Be a Nurse? Should You Go into Personnel Work? Should You Be a Salesman? and even *Should You Enter the Clergy?* Now that automation is wiping out many traditional jobs, these are fields which people, especially young persons, will have to investigate. Similarly, the Metropolitan Life Insurance Company issues pamphlets dealing with the problems of society and the people's welfare.

Another instance of the business world taking account of the age of new leisure is found in the vast enterprise of developing housing. New methods of industrial production make obsolete the practice of concentrating workers' living quarters and factories in crowded cities. In fact, many plants are now being established in wide-open spaces beyond congested areas. Real-estate developers have actualized entirely new concepts of community living, with ample consideration given to pleasant surroundings, the enjoyment of sunshine and fresh air, and the needs of modern family living. Leisure planning is much in evidence. Space in newly developed villages is reserved for libraries and other cultural centers. To please the millions of golfers, neighborhood courses are incorporated into the overall community layout.

Society's Approach to Retirement Leisure

Under the gentle prodding of health and welfare organizations, society is becoming more conscious of a special kind of leisure group, namely, the 17 million people in the United States over 65. This group is destined to grow larger. The Organization for Economic Cooperation and Development states in one of its studies: "It is predicted that between 1960 and 1970 the life expectancy for men will be lengthened by three years (to 69 years) and that the population over 65 years of age will increase by 25 percent (to 20 million)."

People in this group are known by various euphemisms,

44

such as senior citizens or members of Golden Age clubs. Designated "senior," they are a group far from senile. In the *This Week* magazine article "Better Lives for Older People," Martin A. Berenzin, M. D., reported that "only about five percent cannot care for themselves because of organic and/or mental illness." The enjoyment of leisure is for these people a definite possibility.

Because of various interacting economic and social reasons, retirement comes sooner for men and women in industry, business, and the professions. The usual age for withdrawing from active service is 65. Some employees, of course, quit work sooner. Before long, 60 may be the work-termination age for many workers.

Early retirement is joined by another fact, namely, that people in the over-65 bracket live longer. Around the turn of the century (1900) the average man could expect to spend three years in retirement. By midcentury statistics pointed to a six-year retirement period. If the longer-life trend continues, the average 65-year-old man, by A. D. 2000, can look forward to nine more years of life.

Longevity — the longer lifespan — results from better living conditions, improved diets, preventive medicine, the conquest of many diseases, and better medical care for the aged. Both gerontology (the scientific study of the phenomena of old age) and geriatrics (the branch of medicine dealing with the diseases of old age) are contributing toward making life both possible and more pleasant. We have fewer older people with "tired blood," thanks to *materia medica* better than the widely peddled patent medicines, and thanks also to the determination of older people to stay active. The net result of people retiring sooner and living longer is this: a large, still-growing element of our population inherits abundant leisure and possesses mental and physical energy to enjoy it.

What is society doing to help these people? Better still, what is it doing to help retired individuals to help themselves? The American Medical Association, through its 10-year-old Committee on Aging, issues informal pamphlets and sponsors regional conferences to educate people on the facts of retirement and old age and, in one writer's words, "on the need for a philosophy concerning leisure in an aging population."

Many municipalities, in cooperation with social agencies, sponsor senior center programs to assist elderly folk in the use of free time. A firsthand account of such a program comes in a Christmas letter from Mrs. Pauline K., who lives alone in an apartment on Linda Street in San Francisco. In a sense, this woman is retired, being the widow of a man who worked many years for the Union Pacific in North Platte, Nebr. How does she, over 70 years old, keep contentedly busy? She occasionally visits with her children in other parts of the country, but her stay is temporary. Leisure problems have to be worked out where her home is — in San Francisco. There she helps out a family with baby-sitting. A special lifesaver, by her account, is the 700-member center in Aquatic Park. The senior center, open four days a week and on Sunday afternoons, offers a program of crafts and fellowship. During the summer chartered buses take the members on day trips.

Society helps the retired and aged the most when it makes them feel needed and wanted. In so doing it does itself a favor, for many in the 50s, 60s, and 70s are at the peak of their intellectual powers. Also physical strength remains for public and private services.

According to a *Time* report, psychologists Willard A. Kerr of the Illinois Institute of Technology and Ward C. Halstead of the University of Chicago tested over 400 executives of an average age of 52, to determine how age affects mental ability. The results were: "Among the men in their 50s, they found no changes that were inevitable. Some of the men in their 60s and 70s showed a loss of memory, reasoning, and decision-making power, but many did not. Most of the group of 424 aging executives showed as much mental agility as a bunch of medical students averaging 25 years old." The *Time* article added: "Any decline of mental powers with age, the psychologists conclude, is more likely to result from the brain's getting too little rather than too much work."

Medicine, Psychiatry, and Religion

To the team of consultants concerned about channeling leisure into constructive uses we must add representatives of the healing arts, particularly psychiatrists. The latter are equipped to help people where excessive leisure hurts them the most — in their inner selves. Some need counsel and aid in adjusting emotionally to the circumstance of waning working hours and increasing off-time.

Our focus here is not on what individual psychiatrists do in their private dealings with patients, but on the awareness of the profession of psychiatry, as part of our society, vis-a-vis the leisure situation. On that score it is significant that the American Psychiatric Association has formed a standing committee for the study of leisure. The committee, under the chairmanship of Dr. Paul Haun, is keeping abreast of development in order to bring psychiatric skills to bear on the emotional aspects of widespread leisure.

One writer in the medical field has suggested the "mobilization of religion, industry, psychiatry, education, and recreation" to deal with leisure problems. The comment prompts the questions, here posed only for preliminary consideration: Is religion, with the spiritual resources for soul healing at its command, involved in the national round-table discussion on leisure? How much of a counseling role shall it play? Is religion just another leisure-time interest? The *Christianity Today* (Jan. 31, 1964) editorial, "The Christian Use of Leisure," reports: "In an exhaustive study of the problem of leisure in British life by R. Seebohm Rowntree and G. R. Lavers (*English Life and Leisure*, Longman, Green and Co., 1951), religion is treated along with the cinema, the stage, broadcasting, dancing, and reading, as a leisure-time pursuit." Can the church be satisfied to be removed to so peripheral a position?

At a conference on "Leisure and the Recreation of Man," held early in 1964 at Augsburg College, Minneapolis, Dr. Martin E. Marty envisioned a much more important role for Christianity with respect to the "inner soul sickness" that leisure brings to people. He declared, according to a Religious News Service release: "The problem of these people is that they have not learned that leisure, to be creative, must have a source and a purpose. . . . The classic Protestant definition of happiness is enjoyment of God as revealed in Jesus Christ."

The approach of Christian theology to the leisure question remains to be explored in the following portion of this book.

4

LEISURE, WORK
AND THE LORDSHIP OF CHRIST

Is leisure a burden or a blessing? We face not so much an "either-or" as a "both-and" proposition. Coexistence rather than a clear-cut alternative seems to be indicated. Brightbill speaks of leisure as both "the pillar and problem of our scientific culture." Social scientists consider the question and find in the progression of free time the potentiality of an incredible boon to mankind and, simultaneously, the threat of "barren boredom." From the viewpoint of Christian theology, the same possibility is seen to exist, with the difference that conclusions, one way or the other, are reached by other criteria.

Because Christian theology is strongly committed to a doctrine of man as sinner and saint, that is, a doctrine in which the sinfulness of man by nature and the spiritual reconstruction of the Christian by divine grace are cardinal truths, it approaches the pro-and-con discussion of leisure by taking a hard look at the person himself.

Material things, environments, impersonal factors, and external contingencies as they pertain to leisure are of secondary importance. From the Christian viewpoint there is little to be said on whether *leisure* is intrinsically good or not, for like money, guns, or liquor it is neutral. There is much to be said on whether the *individual,* in leisure situations, is using or misusing his personal talents, capacities, and potentialities. The question "Is leisure a burden or a blessing?" hinges on such prior questions as "Who is man?" "What self-image does he have?" "Is he a burden or a blessing to himself?"

Man a Problem to Himself

In *Death of a Salesman* Arthur Miller puts this line into the mouth of Willy Loman's son, who speaks it at the grave of his ill-fated father: "He never knew who he was." It is the loss of self-identity, a fact sometimes skillfully camouflaged but always there, that contemporary playwrights, novelists, and poets have been shouting from the housetops. People without moral and spiritual orientation are portrayed as "the hollow men." In the way they use leisure they expose to outward view the hollow center developing in people of our Western culture.

Twentieth-century man, affluent and self-assured, may plunge into a round of leisure-time activities, even debaucheries, but cannot thereby fill the yawning spiritual void in his heart. In his *A Preface to Morals* Walter Lippmann declares that modern man "has become involved in an elaborate routine of pleasures, and they do not seem to amuse him very much." People become blasé as thrill after thrill loses its tang, with the palling of natural sex pleasures marking their final defeat in the hedonistic adventure.

A deluxe leisure colony is Palm Springs, a plush community which *Newsweek* (April 6, 1964), in its standing "Life and Leisure" feature, describes as "that opulent sand pile in the southern California desert." This would-be oasis, according to the account, has much social gloss: exclusive clubs, spas, swimming pools equipped with devices which create tiny invigorating whirlpools, and links "where golfers now course-hop by helicopter." Even the jailhouse is air-conditioned. The surroundings everywhere are superb, but not all is happiness. Said the *Newsweek* writer: "Ennui is the prevailing mood." At the head of his story he quoted these lines from Alfred Tennyson's "The Lotus-Eaters": Palm Springs is

> *a land*
> *In which it seemed always afternoon . . .*
> *Dark faces pale against that rosey flame,*
> *The mild-eyed melancholy Lotus-eaters came.*

In consequence of his loss of God and self, modern man frequently finds galling boredom in what he does, whether alone or in the company of companions as surfeited as he. This is the shared ennui which Jean-Paul Sartre so poignantly sketches in his play, *No Exit*. For the trapped occupants in Sartre's imaginary hell, time drags endlessly. The "misery loves company" adage notwithstanding, they loathe each other's presence. More leisure, when it is part of depersonalizing tendencies so rife in our century, only accentuates man's lack of self-identity. Free time and free-time diversions become ruinous boomerangs. They don't amuse any longer.

In "Boredom, Not Poverty, Cause of Juvenile Delinquency," a penetrating article published in the Vancouver *Sun* (Nov. 15, 1962), Arthur Miller applies a sharp critique to our society when he writes: "Boredom is the theme of so many of our novels, our plays, and especially our movies in the past twenty years, and is the hallmark of society as a whole. People no longer seem to know why they are alive; existence is simply a string of near-experiences marked off by periods of stupefying spiritual and psychological stasis, and the good life is basically an amused one." Turning the boredom theme to delinquent youths, as products of such a society, he continues: "They are drowning in boredom. School bores them, preaching bores them, even television bores them. . . . To give it even the dignity of cynicism run rampant is also over-elaborate."

Would an improved social environment help? Not altogether, Miller thinks, for this approach does not go deep enough to the roots of the problem. He maintains that "delinquency is not the kind of 'social problem' it is generally thought to be. That is, it transcends even as it includes the need for better housing, medical care, and the rest. It is our most notable and violent manifestation of social nihilism."

Miller proceeds in his analysis: "There are a few social theorists who look beyond poverty and wealth, beyond the time when men will orient themselves to the world as breadwinners, as accusers of money-power. They look to the triumph of technology, when at least in some countries the physical struggle to survive will no longer be the spine of existence. Then, they say, men will define themselves through varying 'styles of life.' With struggles solved, nature tamed and abundant, all that will be left to do will be the adornment of existence, a novel-shaped swimming pool, I take it, or an outburst of artistic work. It is not impossible, I suppose. Certainly a lot of people are already living that way — when they are not at their psychiatrists. But there is still a distance to go before life's style matters very much to most of humanity in comparison to next month's rent."

What is really at the bottom of boredom? Miller attributes it to "technology destroying the very concept of man as a value in himself." Again, "There is, in a word, a spirit gone." To restore life to meaningful existence, he holds, is "to reach for the spirit again."

People in whom the moral and spiritual hollowness of our culture becomes incarnate easily succumb to a sense of supreme frustration. A new school of psychiatry holds that the nothingness feeling not only creeps over people like an uncomfortable, chilling pall but goes so far as to make them emotionally sick, so sick that psychotherapy is needed. The mere thought of nothingness is unbearable. Man is not so constituted as to remain happy and healthy with thoughts of nihilism in his mind.

Human nature, like nature in general, abhors a vacuum. If God is dead, as Nietzsche has taught atheistic existentialists of our time to say, other gods rise up to occupy the vacated place. In our age they are the M-M gods, Mammon and Marxism. In their retinue are all the deities of reviving paganism: Bacchus, the god of drink, Morpheus, the god of drugs, Astarte, the goddess of sex, and all the rest. All the while, people are not really getting what they seek. Basic human needs remain unsatisfied.

Add leisure to the frustration formula, and one can expect reenactments of Samuel Beckett's drama, *Waiting for Godot,* on the stages of individual lives. The plot runs thin: Ragged men wait wearily for a Mr. Godot who never shows up. That is what the play is all about, and that is also what many lives are all about. Leisure in a cultural setting in which God fails to come on stage only heightens the meaninglessness of life. It brings into sharper focus the fact that people who do not know who they are, where they came from, why they are here, what their place is in the divine plan of things, and where they are going are a burden to themselves. And their leisure is a burden because of it.

The need for a theological basis on which to build all

of life is painfully evident. Not leisure, but human nature presents the problem. This fact is not always clearly understood by well-meaning people who seek solutions. In March 1964 the Ad Hoc Committee on the Triple Revolution — cybernation, new nuclear weaponry, and the human rights conflict — presented its report to President Johnson. The committee, consisting of 30 distinguished Americans in many walks of life, foresaw a future in which work is reduced to a minimum. It recommended, on the basis of this supposition, that provision be made for "every individual and every family to receive an adequate income as a matter of right."

Just how this goal was to be achieved, the committee was not prepared to say. An even more serious omission was its failure to see that adjustment to revolutionary changes begins not with the economic system but with persons. In commenting editorially on this report, *Christianity Today* (April 10, 1964) raised the theological issue concerning man. It said: "These momentous problems cannot be adequately discussed without reference to certain theological implications, among which the nature of man himself is paramount."

The Liability of Partial Goals

Evaluating the leisure issue as onus or bonus affords insights when it is related to goals by which men live. The trouble with aims in life is that they are sometimes half right and half safe. In one of His parables Jesus spoke of a man who after a successful harvest planned a life of leisure. "Take thine ease, eat, drink, and be merry," the would-be country gentleman told himself. He had achieved one goal, namely, the amassing of treasures on earth. In failing to relate his objective properly to the higher goal of being "rich toward God," his achievement was incapable of bringing peace to the soul. His leisure, had he lived to experience it, could not have led to personal enjoyment.

A person who cannot see beyond the created good of this world and, on a lower level, beyond man-made "goods," leaves out of purview his highest good in God. His objective in life because of the limitations of his spiritual vision is faulty and insufficient. Personal interests, the quest of culture for its own sake, even altruism and humanitarianism, are partial ends when separated from the love of God. The basic deficiency universally evident in the "cut flower" nature of our secularized society lies in its detachment from spiritual roots. Life is lived on a horizontal plane without reference to the vertical. It is all earth and no heaven; all man and no God. Human love is expected to excel apart from God, who first loved us. Modern man falters in marriage, social life, human relations, civil rights because, under optimum conditions, he aspires to the love of the neighbor without loving God. It is the age-old fallacy of lifting the Golden Rule out of its theological context and setting it up as a goal of life without benefit of spiritual motivation.

Limited goals in life deeply influence man's use of leisure. They are in many instances the determining factors in decision making as to the apportionment of time for work and for leisure. Some invest their leisure in second, or "moonlight" jobs. If their reason is to gain more wealth for the sake of wealth, they evince a vision by which only a segment of life's goal is apparent to them. If leisure means nothing more than fun time, as hedonists measure fun, it bespeaks the individual's enslavement to the great American god Fun. Because of such a commitment, time for diversion is no longer permissive; it is a compulsive time, a time of servitude.

The setting of partial goals prompts people, in academic jargon, to major in minors, to confuse extracurricular with curricular affairs. This error in value judgments, too, casts shadows on the utilization of leisure. It raises the suspicion that the person in question is in all of life not nearly living up to his potential. The dubiously motivated woman who left a sizable estate to her pet cats and thereby involved her relatives in costly court action is a case in point. The love she might have exercised on human beings to relieve poverty, misery, ignorance, and sickness was wholly lavished on lesser creatures. Pets are fine, but they are not persons. We can thrill to Charles M. Schulz's best-selling cartoon book, *Happiness Is a Warm Puppy,* for a pet animal brings leisure-time delight to children and adults. It is quite another thing to blow a legitimate pastime or hobby all out of proportion and make it the prop of one's prime happiness.

For man, in work and in leisure, to settle for too little has aspects of an undeveloped sense of stewardship. It is a near tragedy when a person with the talent of a concert violinist takes up the ukelele instead. To put it more vividly, as one writer has done, it would be both a letdown and a waste of talent for the Boston Symphony Orchestra to assemble on stage before an expectant house, tune up its instruments, and then play "Pop Goes the Weasel." The bane of partial goals and the liability of a low-level outlook on life make the massing of leisure an unrealized treasure for the spiritually immature.

Preoccupation with Trivia

The pursuit of inconsequential interests can be a proper leisure activity, on the assumption that it fulfills one of the purposes of leisure: rest, or disengagement from life's duties. What causes concern about preoccupation with trifles is the value system of many Americans according to which marginal affairs are made life's main objective. When people are mixed up as to the importance and unimportance of what they do, they invariably seek self-images in activities, social or otherwise, which for the moment pay the premium of popular approval or acclaim. So it happens that interests and pastimes perfectly proper for leisure — and normally to be pursued only for leisure — are taken out of that setting and magnified into life's primary missions.

The use of leisure to these ends frequently occurs in closely-knit communities where people jockey for social position. Such places, among others, are the campuses of colleges and universities, and fraternities and sororities as smaller social worlds within these communities. We mention campuses, not because they are different from society as such, but precisely because they mirror the attitudes of society as the larger institution mothering them.

In *Conscience on Campus* Waldo Beach has written an incisive chapter entitled "The Morality of the Social World." He discusses the rounds of extracurricular activities — the sideshows — and finds that they are all too often "the centers of attraction." He adds: "At least there is much more heat and excitement about extracurricular than about curricular affairs." He describes a mixed-up young man in these terms: "He is terribly busy; but if the truth be known, his real campus would be a squirrel cage, in which he is running away from himself. He is 'distracted from distraction by distraction.' With an anarchy of aims, he is caught in the tyranny of trifles. He says 'yes' to everything, college time is frittered away in small matters."

Turning to feminine counterparts on campus, Harry C. Bredemeier and Jackson Toby, in *Social Problems in America,* give us this portrait of coeds likewise confused as to the relative merits of studies and the social whirls of leisure time: "The factors which appear to be important for girls are good clothing, a smooth line, ability to dance well, and popularity as a date. The most important of these factors is the last, for the girl's prestige depends upon dating more than anything else; here as nowhere else nothing succeeds like success."

For every instance cited from the world of youth there is a counterpart from adult society. Fathers and mothers, too, are caught in a system that cannot distinguish between what is primary, secondary, tertiary, and so on down the line. All too often, what is proper for leisure and therefore a side attraction, is lifted out of that context and held up as a symbol of life's chief aims. Only a theology based on the new life in Jesus Christ can redeem men from the tyranny of trifles and set them free for childhood under God.

Guilt Feelings About Leisure

Keeping work and leisure in right perspective is difficult for some Americans because of previous training which blesses the one and discountenances the other. Guilt feelings about leisure, with their roots to some extent in religious teaching, are especially significant from a theological viewpoint. Americans are heirs to a philosophy of work which, according to Max Weber's celebrated essay, "The Protestant Ethic and the Spirit of Capitalism," is compounded of the Calvinistic emphasis on the doctrine of election and capitalistic initiative. The Puritans supposedly brought the "all work — no play" philosophy to the new world. W. R. Forrester, in *Christian Vocation,* recalls how many writers "have emphasized the way in which Puritanism has been largely responsible for industrial development, for it has sent men wholeheartedly into affairs with an ascetic assiduity and concentration, and made them 'religious in it,' spare-living, hard-thinking, straight-dealing, giving 'the more diligence to make their calling and election sure' (2 Peter 1:10)." Others have credited (or blamed) Thomas Carlyle, as philosopher of the Industrial Revolution, for the "work alone is noble" emphasis.

The Protestant work ethic is enshrined in our early American literature. *Poor Richard's Almanac,* edited by Benjamin Franklin in Revolutionary War days, frequently reflected bits of the philosophy of hard work. For a person to get ahead, Horatio Alger fashion, it was necessary for him to concentrate on work and cut out play. Strenuous work and thrift were blessed by many pulpits. John Wesley's notable "money sermon," with its "Earn all you can," "Save all you can," and "Give all you can," predicated industry, frugality, and generosity on the virtue of work, for it was only through relentless effort that financial resources were acquired. The Protestant work ethic was good frontier religion.

Such preachments and practices, of course, entailed a plus and a minus. The plus is represented in the high material accomplishments of America's pioneers in converting a wilderness into a civilized country. The minus involved the undue exaltation of toil to the suppression of leisure-time activities by which mind and spirit live. The gospel of hard work as the royal road to success often issued in cultural impoverishment and anti-intellectualism as other common phenomena of the frontier. The ban of leisure and of theoretical "book learning" go hand in hand when work is made the sovereign virtue.

In the context of early-period literature and preaching, work is largely *physical* labor. Manual toil is what people in an agrarian, preindustrial era had mostly to do. Consequently the praise of work is the praise of muscular work. Noble is the man in Longfellow's "The Village Blacksmith," for his "face is wet with honest sweat." He has no debts; no buying on credit for him. He is beholden to no man. He can face the whole world squarely. What has gotten him this enviable position? His physical labor, done by brawny arms "as strong as iron bands."

Longfellow, Whittier, Franklin, and other early Americans have been our teachers. Their works are classics which children still read in school. The Protestant work ethic undergirding these writings continues to inform the American conscience. Now in the age of leisure, which seems to negate the virtue of work, it is no surprise that many find themselves in a moral dilemma. Americans on whom free time is forced are considerably shocked by a reversal of values in which work is exchanged for involuntary leisure. Their shock is something like the jolt experienced by the passengers of a forward-moving car which is suddenly thrown into reverse. It does not seem right to be sitting around. Leisure is here, but many cannot enjoy it for reason of conscience. It makes them feel guilty not to be doing something worthwhile during long time-off periods.

Partly underlying this scruple is the belief that leisure is the same as the sins of idleness and sloth. Josef Pieper states that to a proletarian or worker-oriented society leisure "is another word for laziness, idleness, and sloth." What are the facts in the case? According to the Bible, leisure as such does not involve anything sinful. Like rest, it comes to people as something earned. It is a very proper thing, a gift of God to be enjoyed. The example of Jesus is helpful here. Our Lord did the works which His Father gave Him to do. But He also observed periods of leisure. When fondling little children, attending social gatherings, resting, or sleeping in the boat while the disciples toiled, He was not being lazy, neglectful, or slothful. The Gospels (Matt. 14:13; Matt. 17:1; Mark 6:31; Luke 9:28) report His retreats to mountains and isolated places for undisturbed rest. Jesus in His life exemplified the propriety of setting aside time for prayer, reflection, and the re-creation of inner life. By His own example and by His explicit charge to the disciples: "Come ye yourselves apart into a desert place, and rest awhile," He safeguarded leisure against the suspicion of indolence. Guilt feelings about leisure are a burden which His modern disciples may confidently discard.

Leisure an Indirect Blessing

The heavy emphasis on work which characterized the past had the possible effect of so immersing people in daily toil that they had neither the time nor inclination to reflect on the deeper meaning of life. Work offered not only occupation but also preoccupation, not only a way of life but also a way to escape true spirituality. With the occupation removed, it is likely that more people will be brought into confrontation with spiritual issues on whose solution their greater happiness depends.

Leisure moments worked out that way for the profligate youth in Christ's parable of the Prodigal Son. As long as he was preoccupied with his major interest of enjoying life materially, he could successfully avoid coming to grips with the facts of his life. After the false props were removed, the young man, in hours of disengagement, "came to himself." He could then begin rebuilding his life on strong spiritual foundations.

In leisure, 20th-century man may return to a consideration of truths which he was able to dodge as long as work possessed him. In the *Pulpit Digest* (March 1963) article, "The Ministry to Persons in a Time of Social Change," Roger L. Shinn considers this a possibility. He writes: "Someone — I think it was Thorsten Veblen — once observed that man's need to work for a living had saved him from the necessity of asking the most important questions of all. That form of salvation may not be with us long. Our fabulously productive economy lets men make a living with less time and concentration than in former ages. The further we go in satisfying man's economic needs, the more obvious some of his other become.

In an affluent society many men will be haunted by the question: 'What will it profit a man if he gains the whole world and forfeits his life?' The answer to that question has not been modified by social change."

Toward Realizing the Blessings of Leisure

Pieper holds that a deep religious basis underlies leisure and culture, namely, worship. He writes: "Culture depends for its very existence on leisure, and leisure, in its turn, is not possible unless it has a durable and consequently living link with the *cultus,* with divine worship." Speaking of leisure as "celebration," he states in a later reference: "If celebration is the core of leisure, then leisure can only be made possible and indeed justifiably upon the same basis as the celebration of a feast: and that formation is *divine worship.*"

In this discussion we prefer to relate leisure to a concept wider and more functional than Christian cultus or formal worship — Christian vocation.

Work and leisure are important elements in the concept of Christian vocation. In seeking to demonstrate why this is so, we attach two significant notes to Christian vocation: (1) Far more than one's job, in fact, one's total Christianity, is meant by this term; (2) Christian vocation is discharged not only in church but also — and principally — in the world.

The Meaning of Christian Vocation

If a man is asked: "What is your vocation?" he is apt to reply: "I am a farmer," "I am a businessman," "I am an engineer." Since there are some 30,000 job classifications, he might give that many answers to inquiries concerning the nature of his job or professional work. These answers frame the idea of vocation in a narrow sense. The concept of Christian vocation, on the other hand, embraces all aspects of Christian life and is as wide a label as the spiritual priesthood of believers. Thus not only work but also leisure is a phase of Christian vocation in this sense.

Vocation refers to the Christian's divine call and calling. It is, first, the call to faith sounded out by the Holy Spirit through the proclamation of the Gospel. This call both invites and empowers the sinner to place his full confidence in the redemption of Jesus Christ. Faith makes him a partaker of Christ's reconciliation and a member of the Kingdom of Grace. Through Baptism the life of grace is begun. Regenerated by water and the Word, the person is called to be an heir of salvation and is sealed as such.

Christian vocation in its fullest sense, as Alfred P. Klausler stresses in *Christ and Your Job*, bespeaks "the action on the part of God calling persons or mankind into a state of salvation or union with Him." What are the consequences? Klausler continues: "Thus it is that because God has extended this unmerited mercy to us, we are called by Him. We belong to the category of the called of God. We belong to a glorious fellowship. You are God's 'chosen generation,' His 'royal priesthood,' His 'holy nation,' His 'peculiar people' — all the old titles of God's people now belong to the Christians." Spiritual priests have not only these honorable titles but also functions, or divine offices. The function stressed by Peter in his epistle is that they exhibit and celebrate the praises of God before the world.

The call to total discipleship includes, of course, that phase of Christian vocation which in everyday language is known as one's job, one's work, or one's position in life as father, mother, son, or daughter. From the divine call it follows that Christians' job, work, or position is a divine calling, whatever it may be. In the "Work and Property" chapter of his *Ethics of Decision* George W. Forell writes: "The particular character of the work makes little difference indeed. Through faith it is possible to see not only the more spectacular professions of the surgeon, the statesman, the pastor, and the missionary as avenues of Christian service, but also the truck driver, the riveter, the clerk, and the janitor. A job is a calling not by virtue of its own inherent character but by virtue of the Christian understanding of the jobholder. Every work done to the glory of God and in the service of our fellowman is a Christian calling."

Martin Luther contributed much toward restoring the high estimate of the Christian's daily work as a God-pleasing calling. Gustav Wingren, in *Luther on Vocation,* restates Luther's position thus: "Vocations differ among us: farmers, fishers, and men of all orders who handle creation's wares, carry God's gifts to their neighbors, even if their purpose is not always to serve. God is active in this. . . . God Himself will milk the cows through him whose vocation that is. He who engages in the lowliness of his work performs God's work, be he lad or king."

One finds people, even Christians, who are under the impression that the job is secular and has nothing to do with one's Christianity. They have the idea of a bureau with separate drawers marked "My Work" and "My Christianity." The job, however, has everything to do with one's faith, for through it the Christian serves his Lord and shows forth His praises before the world.

The Arena for Christian Vocation

A common misconception has it that Christians exercise their divine calling only in church or only by engaging in Christian worship, works of Christian charity, and other religious activities under church auspices. Christians do indeed assemble in the house of God for worship, spiritual nurture, and the mutual exercise of love. But that is not the whole of their function as Christ's witnesses. The God they serve is not boxed in within the four walls of temples made with hands. He is the Lord of the universe. Consequently God's children bring their Christianity to the outside world and there show forth His praises by what they are, say, and do.

The world is the arena where Christian faith is appropriately proclaimed and practiced through vocation. Emphasis on the exercise of faith within culture rather than alongside it is a Reformation heritage and is as timely now as it was then. Luther's position on Christian vocation included this accent. H. Richard Niebuhr writes in *Christ and Culture:* "More than any great Christian leader before him, Luther affirmed the life in culture as the sphere in which Christ could and ought to be followed." Similarly Harold J. Grimm, in an essay entitled "Lutheranism as a Cultural Force," holds: "Luther probably demonstrated a greater affirmation of the things of this world than any other reformer. His writings abound with references to the proper enjoyment of God's gifts."

With culture in the Western world going rapidly to seed in secularism and a new humanism from which God is excluded, Christian people need to extend themselves in its behalf, revitalizing it by active participation in it. As bearers of the Christian heritage they are called for such a time as this to witness to the Word of God by voice and vocation. The shock troops of our Lord's "salvation army" are Christian people whose daily work takes them into direct encounter with the spiritually uncommitted. They are cheek by jowl with secularists, materialists, and that whole crew known as "post-Christian" people.

Christ's Lordship over World and Church

Christian vocation, as both status and function with a "this-worldly" cast, corresponds to the Lordship of Jesus Christ over creation. In Paul's words, Christ is over "all things created, that are in heaven and that are in earth, visible and invisible." As subjects, Christians follow their calling in this world because Christ, as King and Creator, asserts His sovereignty there. Nature and culture — the whole range of empirical and nonempirical creation — is the sphere He claims and reclaims for His rule. His followers in the world at any moment in history do not themselves establish that rule. They merely announce the fact of its existence from the beginning. Early explorers who first arrived in new lands claimed the territory for their king by planting their standards on it. Before this, of course, the king's rule was not in effect. Christ's authority over the kingdoms of this world and the whole realm of nature predates the arrival of the first Christians in any virgin territory. Christ is Lord by virtue of being the Word in the beginning and the Creator of the universe. The earth on which men build cultures and civilizations is Christ's, and His is the fullness thereof.

The Lordship of Jesus Christ extends also over the church, or the Kingdom of Grace, as His spiritual realm. God gave His Son "to be the Head over all things to the church, which is His body, the fullness of Him that filleth all in all." In the holy Christian church, the communion of saints, Christ is Lord by virtue of His atonement and resurrection. By these redemptive acts the incarnate Son of God became the Savior of His body, the church. Now ascended into heaven, He continues His gracious rule in the church through the Word of the Gospel and the sacraments. All who acknowledge Him as Lord and Savior are made members of the church, to be nourished in faith, grow in fellowship with Him and one another, worship and serve Him, and carry out His will to go into all the world and preach the Gospel to every creature.

Under the Lordship of Jesus Christ over world and church, all His disciples, in the discharge of their vocation, are involved in the work of two kingdoms, the Kingdom of Power and the Kingdom of Grace. Split personalities and bilevel loyalties, however, are avoided because they live under the unit dominion of Christ. Christians as citizens in two realms are subject to one Lord. As they pass from the church, where faith is nurtured, to the world, where faith is exercised, they are not crossing borders separating two regimes or governments. The Berlin wall and other barriers dividing West Germany from East Germany do demarcate two regimes. None can be a citizen in both countries, because they are under two governments. Christians active in church and world are under the one government of Christ. As they follow their calling from one realm to the other, they are like British Commonwealth citizens going from England to Scotland, both members of the United Kingdom and both subject to one government.

From their base as members of the Kingdom of Grace, Christians serve as their Lord's workmen and witnesses in the world. As members of His body, the church, they receive strength, motivation, and direction to walk worthy of the vocation wherewith they are called. Under Christ as Head of the body they are united for their common task. No Christian is detached, to live for himself and by himself. Each one is enabled to live for Christ and for the total community of persons constituting His body. The love of God imparted in the kingdom of grace is the incentive for being Christ's people in the world. In his *Being a Christian in Today's World* Walter Leibrecht writes: "It is the divine compassion and love for man and his world that drives us into the world. And it is the same love, His grace, which makes Christian existence in this world possible."

Christian Vocation and the Blessings of Leisure

The concept of Christian vocation under the Lordship of Jesus Christ puts meaning, purpose, and joy into work. By the same token it invests leisure with a sense of divine blessing. Christians do their work to God's glory. In the same measure do they glorify God by rest and leisure. Both work and recreation, toil and rest, stand under His benediction. Everything that serves the pleasurable leisure of God's people is the gift of Him "who giveth us richly all things to enjoy." When vacation travels take them into the great outdoors, they find it possible to engage in thankful contemplation of God's wonderful creation, and join in the psalmist's exultation: "The works of the Lord are great, sought out of all them that have pleasure therein."

The works of nature, says Paul, "God hath created to be received with thanksgiving of them which believe and know the truth." The apostle continues to urge the point: "Every creature of God is good . . . if it be received with thanksgiving." Luther, too, was convinced that God "makes all creation help provide the comforts and necessities of life — sun, moon, and stars in the heavens, day and night, air, fire, water, the earth and all that it brings forth, birds and fish, grain and all kinds of produce." Vacationing, camping, hiking, hunting, fishing — whatever a Christian does in leisure — he receives God's gifts with thanksgiving and counts them blessings.

Leisure is a liability for "hollow men." All the evils in the B-zone — burden, boredom, barrenness, bane — descend on people swamped with free time if they don't know who they are, whose they are, and why they are in this world. For "full men," that is, for those who, in Paul's words, "know the love of Christ" and are "filled with the Spirit," leisure brings other B-zone effects: blessings, benefits, bonuses. That is because leisure is fitted into the framework of the Christian faith. Work time, free time, leisure, leisure-time activities, hobbies, and avocations — all are aspects of Christian vocation or the spiritual priesthood of believers.

Under the Lordship of Jesus Christ the great distinctions many want to make between work and leisure, as though one were God's will and the other not, all but disappear. To a Christian finding delight to serve his Lord both work and leisure are pleasant, with sometimes the one blending into the other. The cobbler in the song *Le Petit Cordonnier* ("The Little Shoemaker"), carried his work into leisure hours because he was doing a deed of love. He was making exquisite dancing shoes for a little girl of whom he was very fond. So he

> *. . . tapped and he stitched,*
> *For his fingers were bewitched,*
> *And he sewed a dream*
> *Into every seam.*

Everything that constitutes Christian vocation: work and play, labor and leisure, worship and rest, is tendered to Christ as a love offering. It is therefore delightful, for love prompts it.

5

CHRISTIAN USE OF LEISURE

According to a law of physics, to every action there is a reaction. The principle of cause and effect is in force in the divine relationship between God and His people. The action of God for human salvation, culminating in the incarnation, atonement, and resurrection of His Son Jesus Christ, prompts a reaction in those whom the Holy Spirit has called to faith. The response of Christians to Christ's redemption is love in return, love which is a fruit of the Spirit. John declares: "We love Him because He first loved us."

Christian love proceeds not only in a vertical, or heavenward, direction, in the sense of counterlove to God; it functions also horizontally, coming to many expressions of concern and compassion for fellowmen and leading the person to right action with respect to himself. A force so vital in Christians' lives reveals its excellence in the use of God's gifts in every dimension of stewardship: talent, treasure, and time. The dynamic of love to God and human beings deeply influences a Christian in the use of leisure.

Leisure and the Christian Family

Leisure provides many opportunities for the Christian family to be the community of Jesus Christ in the sanctuary of the home. In free time this fellowship of parents and children with Christ is enabled to come to fullest fruition. It fulfills its image as a microcosm of the communion of saints, as a miniature of the "whole family in heaven and earth" named after the Father of our Lord Jesus Christ. All members were baptized into Christ, to be saved by Him and then to serve Him. Through Him father, mother, brothers, sisters, and grandparents, if this is a three-generation family, are the children of the heavenly Father. All show their response to the love of God in the way they let leisure serve the family's welfare.

Worshipful Response

One form of this response is worship in family devotions with prayers, hymns, and Bible readings. Worship edifies and solidifies the home as nothing else can. It lays the foundation for other undertakings as a group. It is a link with members away from home and with other Christian families. Intervening space is overcome when at given times all assemble in spirit at the Throne of Grace. The unity of Christendom is furthered when family groups in their individual homes coordinate their devotions with the rhythm of the church year or follow a selected series of Bible readings.

There is advantage to having a set time for family devotions. In domestic circles the leisure of evening hours — the lull after evening meals or the time before retiring —

is best suited for joint worship. The momentum of good habits assists in maintaining worship regularity. It helps when everyone in the family knows: "This is the time when we gather for prayers," or "This is the hour when father and mother teach the Word of God."

Worship meaningfully and creatively fostered at home carries over into the family's vacation activities. The leisure of a holiday weekend in the mountains or at a lakeside is ideal for group devotions. Here is a story told by the stewardship editor of a magazine for Christian women:

> A Christian family was vacationing at a lake cottage. As they were enjoying their outdoor meal on Saturday evening, the father asked how they should plan to hold Sunday morning services, since they were at a great distance from a church.
>
> "We could have our church service right here," spoke up Bob, "if we had our hymnbooks."
>
> "I thought of that — and brought our hymnals with me," replied Father.
>
> While the two sons went off into the woods to build a cross, Mother and Sally arranged an altar with candles and flowers. Father planned the order of service with the help of the hymnal, Portals of Prayer, and his Bible.
>
> As the boys finished making a fine cross from the best branches they could find, Bob said, "It is a lot of work getting ready for a worship service, but I don't really mind. We know that God is here too."
>
> The next day there was a new joy for the family worshiping together outdoors. They agreed it was well worth the planning. They knew God was with them.

Family worship is closely related, in nature and purpose, to Sunday worship in church. "We keep holy days so that people may have time and opportunity, which otherwise would not be available, to participate in public worship, that is, that they may assemble to hear and discuss God's Word and then praise God with song and prayer," writes Martin Luther.

Sunday free time, as part of weekend leisure, invites to enjoyable activities on beaches, in resort areas, or on the home premises. It need not, and for most Christian families it does not, keep people from worshiping in church. Elmo Roper, senior partner of Elmo Roper and Associates, reports in *This Week* magazine (Nov. 24, 1963), on the basis of a nationwide survey: "We found that for most Americans, Sunday is a very special day. . . . For nearly half of the people we asked, it is because it's the day when they go to church. For these people, church is not just a habit and it is considerably more than a duty. It is the essential meaning of the day."

How do average American families spend Sunday? Roper goes on: "The typical Sunday might run something like this: Americans will sleep a bit longer on Sunday than the rest of the week. However, 83 percent of the country is up by nine in the morning. . . . Morning is the time for a leisurely breakfast, reading the Sunday paper, and going to church. After dinner, some people take a drive to visit relatives or friends; others just sit around and relax. A few people work around the house or the yard on Sunday. Many get involved in discussions about present family problems and future plans."

At Ease in the Christian Home

The response of the Christian family to the divine gift of leisure is not expressed only in devotional or religious exercises. Leisure is for other things besides praying and meditating on the Word of God. Besides the family altar there are other furnishings in the home for the rightful and God-pleasing use of free time. Easy chairs, beds, and tables remind us of everyday functions we must fulfill. They are for resting, sleeping, eating, or the complete cessation of work. Leisure time at home is for getting out of the harness, for relieving tensions, for finding peace. Luther said on one occation: "We also serve God by doing nothing, in fact, in no way more than by doing nothing." Pieper speaks of the three elements of leisure as "effortlessness, calm, and relaxation."

The usual home appointments indicate what leisure activities are appropriate for Christian families. The reading lamp near a comfortable chair says that leisure is for cultivating acquaintance with good books and magazines. The writing desk in the corner suggests the use of free time for writing letters, making diary entries, or checking on the family budget. There is a niche for the record player or stereo set. Listening to music and playing it are excellent leisure pastimes.

Modern homes are provided with areas especially designed for various activities. Somewhere in the house is a playroom for smaller children, a sewing room or nook for Mother, a hobby workshop for Father, and recreation space for the family as a whole. In common rooms the family does things together. In private rooms individuals can be undisturbed as they read or do homework. Someone has called these features of modern homes the "leisure-time ecologies," that is, architectural means whereby the right environment is created for free-time home functions. The growth of leisure for the family suggests a house structured to accommodate present-day conditions.

The modern home is planned for the leisure-time use of the many media of communications: printed matter, radio, television, telephone, and inter-com systems. To obtain optimum enjoyment from these devices, a few dos and don'ts are needed, also in Christian homes, to set moral and cultural standards. Good books, yes; trashy novels, no. "Rock 'n Roll" radio music — a little of it is plenty. Music in a popular vein, especially symphonic music, now carried mostly by FM radio — let it be played. Gory television shows — a slight twist of the wrist can change the channel. The observance of a few simple rules on the use of the telephone, especially by teen-agers in the home, makes this instrument available when needed. No member will want to be selfish with it, tying up the line with hour-long conversations while others wait or keeping out incoming calls.

The family at leisure keeps its friendships alive by going visiting and receiving visitors. Good friends and faithful neighbors are among life's choicest blessings. We must put forth effort to keep friendships in good repair. To *have* friends, it is necessary to *be* friends. The complaint is frequently made, especially on draggy Sunday afternoons or during long winter evenings: "Why doesn't anybody ever come and visit us?" This may be less a commentary on other people's unfriendliness than it is a confession of one's own failure to go and visit others. Leisure invested in Christian sociability yields dividends in terms of a better social equilibrium for the family and an improved outlook on life.

Leisure and Home Training

The worshipful reaction of Christians to God's gift of more free time manifests itself in the way parents structure the training and education of children for life in the age of leisure. The educational process they choose is informed by insights derived by keeping both the Word of God and the present situation in clear focus. The first educators are the parents, for they mold children in preschool years and continue their influence over them in ensuing years.

The age of leisure is opportune for laying greater emphasis on making a *life* than making a *living*. Parents committed to the Christian faith strive to bring up children for a balanced life, a life in which all personal needs are met and the individual's potential is realized. The plan for building life provides for personal growth in the spiritual, mental, physical, and social dimension, with the understanding, of course, that the child is a whole person and that these types of growth are not compartments but aspects of overall development in whatever order they are stated.

The basic blueprint for Christian growth along the lines indicated is contained in Luke's description of the childhood development of our Lord: "Jesus increased in wisdom and stature and in favor with God and man." A Christian person taking his stance in a culture featuring Space Age explorations, technology, automation, and leisure needs to be well balanced, in Tennyson's lines, answering to the stability of

That tower of strength
Which stood four-square to all
Winds that blew.

Increasing leisure at home opens the door to teaching in which spiritual growth is the object of primary concern. The *area* of such development is defined by Peter when he urges young and old to "grow in grace and in the knowledge of our Lord and Savior Jesus Christ." The *means* for maturation is underscored by the same apostle in a statement included in the introit for the Sunday after Easter (Quasimodogeniti): "As newborn babes, desire the sincere milk of the Word, that ye may grow thereby." By the same token, growth in baptismal grace and closer union with Christ through Holy Communion are inferred. Christ risen from the dead is the *Source* of spiritual growth, for into Him children are baptized. The ideal of *progress* in Christian life is stated by the writer of Hebrews, who seeks to wean maturing Christians from milk diets and put them on "strong meat" as appropriate for "them that are of full age." The concept of *growth together* is expressed in Paul's "Let the Word of Christ dwell in you richly" as a Christian community and in his "teaching and admonishing one another." The presence of leisure as a proper *condition* for the germination of the implanted seed of the Word is implied in Jesus' parable: "So is the kingdom of God, as if a man should cast seed into the ground, and should sleep, and rise night and day, and the seed should spring and grow up."

Total-Person Education

Leisure comes to the advantage of both parents and children in achieving total personal growth, also in knowledge, in "physical fitness," in social responsibilities.

First, mental growth. Quiet leisure time is effectively redeemed in studying and other activities that enhance mental talents. Christians serve God also with the intellectual powers, loving Him with all their minds. They pray, in the words of a song title: "God, Be in My Head." Their song prayer is also: "Take my intellect and use, Every power as Thou shalt choose." For Christians, educational pursuits by young and old are motivated by the desire to minister to Christ and His brethren more competently.

Physical education, as well, has the sanction of Christian teaching, for it involves the care of the body which the Holy Spirit has chosen as His temple. The use of leisure for physical development is a phase of the Christian's thankful response to Christ's redemption of his body. By this exercise believers present "their bodies a living sacrifice, holy, acceptable unto God."

Social growth aids the Christian person in relating himself meaningfully to human society within and without the church. Each one's role in the human-relations area is expedited through social education. That role is more than just a "walk on" part; it is significant participation in the drama of life. It is prompted by Christian love and considered worth all the time and effort spent in rehearsals. Not the individual performance, not the performing star, but "the play is the thing," with the rest of the cast and the audience always kept in mind. The English divine, John Donne, has taught that no man is an island by himself. Barring the recluse or hermit, every person is at least a peninsula connected with the continent of larger society. The fulfillment of Christian fellowship rests on growing "in favor with God and man."

Child Guidance in the Use of Leisure

Home-based Christian education prepares children for the prudential use of leisure. It does this in one of the best ways possible: participation in leisure now. It corrects many mistaken ideas, including the belief that a child can't bear leisure, that all its free time must be spent in active play with neighborhood children. Worth considering is the comment of Sydney J. Harris, a syndicated columnist: "Why must we always assume that children like to be — or should be — together all the time, any more than adults like to be together all the time? A child, perhaps even more than adults, is entitled to its own solitude and its own dream of glory. . . . For some psychological reasons many people feel strangely ill at ease when a child is just sitting around doing nothing, although this is often the best thing a child can do." Parents do well to guide children to finding enjoyment and purposefulness in sometimes solitary leisure situations.

Christian fathers and mothers bring discerning insights to the current emphasis on summer-long camps for children, as well as to park and playground summer programs which are adult-supervised. They consider the situation of organized baseball leagues for boys in which the adult "will to win," at times harbored by managers in the field and by proud dads in the stands, comes to strong vocal expression. They realize that activities planned for children can generate undue pressure for immature lads or become forms of adult regimentation which stifle youthful initiative. The solution is not the abolition of adult interest and leadership, but the striking of a favorable balance between supervision and the children's freewill participation. Christian parents proceed on the conviction that youngsters can begin to assume responsibility for planning their own lives and for exercising options concerning leisure pastimes. They can contribute to the right balance in adult-child relationships by taking part in community programs for children and bringing good insights to the task.

Christian parents offer helpful counsel to children in early teens anent the leisure aspects of social life. Like Paul, they know that it is proper for a child to speak as a child, understand as a child, think as a child, and have the interests of a child. Therefore they do not expect social precociousness. They question whether children should be hurried too soon into adult ways, such as having "dates" when still in grade school or taking adult-style social dancing lessons, particularly if the apparent motive is to use socially refined children as status symbols. Not current social mores of questionable worth, not majority behavior, not peer-group precedents, but principles which assure the total welfare of the child as a child are the deciding factors.

Formal Education

How Christians relate leisure to life is evident from the kind of education parents want their children to receive in school. They will choose, and assist in, that type of training which leads youngsters into an appreciation of Christian vocation and their calling as youthful spiritual priests. This, so Christian parents know, is the best preparation for life possible. Come more leisure and other developments, the children are ready; they are spiritually equipped, not only to take these things in stride, but also to make them serve the purpose for which God has placed His people into the world.

How can the truth of Christian vocation be inculcated? The Supreme Court has ruled that the Christian religion, or any other religion, cannot be formally and expressly exercised in the public schools. The judicial veto does not, however, prevent children from receiving Christian instruction. It is by no means a ban of religion as such, as would be the case in hard-line communistic lands. The Constitution continues to safeguard the free exercise of religion. For Christian education, home, Sunday schools, vacation Bible schools, released-time classes, and Christian day schools exist. Public school children have access to Christian books at home and elsewhere. They are influenced by Christian teachers in city or district schools. No constitutional amendment proposes to screen out the tacit teaching power of the Christian teacher's example and attitude. Emerson can be paraphrased here: What Christian teachers are speaks so loudly that we cannot hear what they say.

Among agencies of Christian education the Christian day school holds a preeminent position, as does also the Christian high school. The strength of this system is that a synthesis of faith and learning is achieved, with faith providing the framework and dynamic of learning. Christian education proposes to put Christ into the center of the curriculum, with the view of putting Him into the pupil's heart. It has been said many times: The heart of Christian education is the education of the heart. Christ-centered education formulates answers to life's all-important questions. It imparts guidance to man in the latter half of the 20th century when, amid the stagger of society from one crisis to another, moral standards are all but vanishing. Christian education both comprehends and transcends knowledge in that it teaches children "to know the love of Christ" and furnishes them "with all the fullness of God."

Christian Youth and Leisure

"Christian youth" is a rather wide label. It covers young people of high school and college age, in short, adolescents and young adults whether in school or working. Does youth have leisure? After the Russians sent Sputnik aloft, students in American high schools and colleges were made to bear heavier scholastic loads, much to the shrinkage of free time. Admiral Rickover, James B. Conant, Robert M. Hutchins, and other commentators on education have asked greater excellence in learning. Yet leisure remains to a greater or lesser degree also for serious students. Its use from a Christian viewpoint merits a succinct discussion.

Students in high school and college find leisure outlets in various types of social activities associated with school. They join social clubs where closer friendships are formed. This is to be encouraged, unless, of course, these clubs foster partisanship and a spirit of snobbery. A good approach to the problem of unwarranted exclusiveness is to work actively for correction, and usually this can best be done by being a positive Christian influence inside the organizations as members and officers.

It is normal for young people to spend leisure time in dating. Much has been said on this phase of social life: whom to date, how deeply dating should be allowed to cut into one's study time and free time, what to do and what not to do on dates, where to go, and the like. These are important questions for young Christians, to consider personally and to discuss with parents and at youth group meetings at church. Our present interest is to include dating in the list of things Christian youth does in good conscience during leisure time. Dating under conditions of propriety is part of social life by which Christian young people interact with others according to instincts God Himself has inscribed into their nature.

Christians on campus take of their free time to participate in extracurricular affairs by which that community of persons benefits. Such affairs include the athletic program, student council, dormitory government, buildings and grounds committee, publication of yearbooks and school newspapers, membership in vocational training groups, as well as activities sponsored by the class. Extracurricular service is an expression of the Christian vocation of studentship.

Apart from the school situation, Christian students in leisure hours are willing to allot time for personal and community services within the range of their aptitudes. An excellent service performed by students at the University of Chicago and other colleges is tutoring socially underprivileged, scholastically retarded school children in submarginal neighborhoods. To keep pupils on the borderline of failure from dropping out of school is to make a positive, constructive contribution toward the inner-city youth problem. Prevention is better than cure. A pupil kept in school and aided in his learning is given a better chance to become a useful member of society.

During summer months many students take jobs to earn money for the continuation of their education. At that, weekends and evenings are mostly free. For nearly every situation in which students find themselves in the summer there is a corresponding full-time or part-time service opportunity. Churches and welfare organizations of a civic nature are willing to engage students for a variety of projects, both on subsistence salaries and a no-pay basis. Work can be done in U. S. inner cities, in foreign lands, and in mission fields at home and abroad. The period of service varies with the nature of the program.

Workers' Rest Periods

Along with their co-workers, Christians on the job enjoy rest periods during noon hours and at other times during the day. This leisure occurs where they work: in market places, industries, city halls and county court houses, cultural centers, noonday luncheon clubs for businessmen, and so forth. In Chicago, as in other cities, many Christian men and women prefer to eat their midday lunches in the company of other Christians. Perhaps once a week they come together for noon meetings to say prayers and receive an inspirational message from the Bible. Many denominations are establishing loop or downtown churches which feature spiritual programs for daytime workers and shoppers.

Christianity is not only a Sunday affair, and Christian fellowship is too glorious a gift of Christ as to be practiced for only an hour in church. In *Life Together* Dietrich Bonhoeffer writes: "Among earnest Christians in the church today there is a growing desire to meet together with other Christians in the rest periods of their work for common life under the Word. Communal life is again being recognized by Christians today as the grace that it is, as the extraordinary, the 'roses and lilies' of the Christian life."

Leisure and Aging Christians

For Christians comes the time to retire from their several income-producing vocations, but Christian vocation in its highest sense continues. They may no longer be practitioners of trades, crafts, and professions, but spiritual priests they are always. With the lengthening of life — through the sixties, the Biblical threescore years and ten, fourscore years, and beyond — gratefulness for God's multiplying blessings increases correspondingly. As life is seen in the perspective of many years, the forgiveness of sins, the promise of life, and gifts of divine grace are the more appreciated. The response to mercies new every morning is the Christian's recognition of the continuing Lordship of Jesus Christ and the dedication of time and talents to Him.

Thanks to various kinds of incomes, the retired and aging are able to enjoy leisure more. There is no cause for the "What shall we eat? What shall we drink? and Wherewithal shall we be clothed?" worries. Over 65 and no longer earning, most people can live reasonably well on their financial resources. As Christians they find joy in being able to continue their giving to the Lord. Thanks to retirement income, they are able to live independently. The need of moving in with the children is eliminated. The three-generation family in one house used to be quite common. According to some family-life consultants, grandparents are better off living in their own homes or apartments. Many modern homes today are not designed to accommodate an extra couple.

The passing of the triple-generation family living under one roof entails both a gain and a loss. The gain is this, that grandparents living in their own home have more privacy. They can set their own style of living. There is less occasion for personality clashes over differences of opinion on cooking, managing the household, or disciplining the children. The loss is reflected in the possible loosening of family solidarity. The presence of grandparents in the home once represented continuity. The child sensed that he was a member of a family tree, with roots, trunk, branches, and leaves. He learned from grandparents many lessons distilled from the wisdom of experience. Also the elderly benefited from associating closely with active family units. They felt they were still in the swim of things and their services were needed.

Financial competence frees the retired and aging from the necessity of being housefast, or from having to live in one place. It gives them the choice of staying put or moving to areas with milder climates. Many retired folk pick up this option and transplant themselves to communities better suited to their health and other personal circumstances. Available to them are planned villages, sometimes operated under Christian auspices, where leisure can be enjoyed in congenial company. Others prefer to spend their retirement in traveling, either in conventional ways or by house trailer.

During retirement Christians have the opportunity to reach self-fulfillment by reading, writing, cultivating new interests, and pursuing spiritual projects directly related to Christian vocation. Many retired persons are heard to say: "We are just as occupied now with things as we were before." In most instances, these are people who had given thought to their retirement in previous years and prepared for it. It is a good idea for everyone in mid-forties and fifties to develop a number of interests up to a point, with the resolve: "These things I will complete when I retire." There are many blessings locked up in books. To discover this wealth in later years, it is good to do some prospecting now by taking trips to libraries and bookstores.

Retired Christians are at leisure to give more meaningful and more literal expression to the ideals of service. The church's senior members can serve their Lord in ways other (and better) than just playing dartball or coming together in church parlors only to chat. God is pleased with Christian fellowship, particularly if it issues in the discharge of the church's mission — Christian evangelism and Christian nurture.

The church itself, as well as its agencies and sub-groups, offers opportunities for members of all ages to serve with their talents, insights, and experiences. It invites the retired banker or window clerk to assist with the financial program, the retired teacher to take over a church class, the retired businessman to offer administrative assistance to pastor and parish.

6

THE MINISTRY OF
THE CHURCH IN A LEISURE CULTURE

The Christian church, as the continuing body of Christ in the world, proclaims the good news of salvation to total persons in a total society. It announces in the presence of abundant human sin the always superabundant grace of God in Jesus Christ. The intent of its mission is to call sinners to repentance, lead them into communion with Christ by faith, and involve them meaningfully in the new life under the Gospel. The tools through which the Holy Spirit accomplishes these purposes in the church are the Word and sacraments. For the creation of faith and its nurture the means are the same and remain the same. By these ordinances of His house Christ equips the church for its mission to the end of time.

Vicissitudes are the order of the day in human culture. Things modern are soon obsolescent, then obsolete. Social revolution follows social revolution. All the while the church is steadily about its task of achieving the spiritual revolution: the reconstruction of human nature through the Gospel. The automation upset, with mass leisure in its wake, is another in a succession of events to which the church directs its ministry. In all crises it is the bearer of God's message to men, not as a social agency using secular tools, but always, as Christ's own institute, renewing the old and creating the new through the means of grace.

Let the Church Be the Church

The church is people, a very special kind of people, with a two-way attachment in their fellowship. In his essay "The Body of Christ" Richard R. Caemmerer states these attachments thus:

1. *The body of Christ is composed of people who are attached to Christ as Head because of His redeeming work and by means of the Gospel of that work.*

2. *The body of Christ is composed of individuals who, through the redeeming work of Christ and His Word, are attached to one another in unity by love.*

As to point one, Robert Meyners, in *Perspectives of a Campus Church,* says much the same as he identifies the church as the "community of those who know themselves to be sinners but who call upon God's grace manifest in Jesus Christ." The sense of community under one Lord Jesus Christ expresses itself in joint worship and in multiple undertakings for mutual edification. The need for identification, both with Christ and with other Christians in some tangible form of fellowship, is immediately evident. Dr. A. B. B. Moore, president of Victoria University, Toronto, writes in the 1964 Social Service Report of the United Church of Canada: "The Church is a community of commitment — a community composed of those whose lives are committed to Christ. Such commitment means membership within a church fellowship and the general acceptance of its doctrines, liturgies, ethics, discipline and service."

In the measure that the church is true to itself can it carry out its mission to the world. As it continues to cherish its self-image as God's own foundation on earth to prepare men for heaven, so is its effectiveness preserved. The church is *in* the world but never *of* the world. In his *Significance of the Church* Robert McAfee Brown recalls Paul's concept of the church, in Moffatt's translation, as "a colony of heaven." He explains: "A colony exists far away from the homeland, but the members give allegiance not just to the colony, but chiefly to the homeland. And the Church as a 'colony of heaven' is thus a foretaste of 'earnest' of what is one day to be true for all."

The church serves the world best by remaining in character as a spiritual entity with spiritual goals. Meyners states: "The church must be itself. The church must be something definite, a recognizable entity, not a vague zone or just another organization. It must have a style that is not identical with that of culture." Again: "The church does no service to secular culture when it loses its identity. It is a gathered community, an *ekklesia,* which means literally the 'called out.' To exist at all the church must be called out of the world. . . . However this does not mean to be 'called away,' to be separate from culture. Rather, it means the fullest possible participation; otherwise to be called out results in irrelevance."

The Church for the World

The church as the people of God understands Peter correctly not only when he describes it as "a chosen generation, a royal priesthood, an holy nation, a peculiar people," but also when he points to its function: ". . . that ye should show forth the praises of Him who hath called you out of darkness into His marvelous light." The awareness of its mission to the world keeps the church from introversion, self-centeredness, and institutionalized contentment. Extroverted toward the world, the church's members, having met for worship and spiritual nurture, then disassemble and disperse on errands of love. In the footsteps of their Lord they go forth as servants to minister to mankind along the highways and byways of mundane life.

The Church and Leisure Culture

The church's proper self-understanding as a servant in the world is a prerequisite for its ministry in a leisure culture. Were the church to consider itself a self-serving institution, it would rest content to marshal its resources only to relieve its own members of the ill effects of leisure. The result would then be a program providing for more senior-citizens centers, more youth centers, more recreation halls, more day nurseries — all for the convenience of its own leisure-burdened parishioners. When the church follows this tack, it becomes a glorified tension-relieving, hand-holding, baby-sitting agency in behalf of itself.

Not a few parishes in suburbs and other metropolitan settings take this route of self-service. Catering to a leisure society, they help members take up the slack of excessive and burdensome free time by placing personnel, programs, and facilities at their disposal. The church, by this approach, is little more than a link in the chain of community organizations for the social outlets of leisure. The road leads to the church's captivity to a leisure culture. The temptation to fit too snugly into the scene and serve as a leisure-time interest must be resisted with fortitude.

The leisure age imposes on the church the need of reexamining its program in the light of what it, as the body of Christ, is and what it should be doing. The church does well to ask: "Are we doing Kingdom work?" Because members have more leisure, it does not follow that they may be summoned to more meaningless activities under parish auspices. The parish is a waster of time when it involves people in trivial "church doings" which have no relation to the primary concerns of the Gospel. With free time multiplying but also life becoming more meaningless, it is time to clear up confusions which are the bane of parish life: doing things just for the sake of doing, doing right things for wrong reasons, and wrong things for right reasons, or not at all doing the things God expects.

When gasoline was in short supply during World War II, motorists were asked to keep this question always in mind: "Is this trip necessary?" Similarly, let the church, from grassroots parishes to denominational headquarters, ask: "Is this meeting necessary?" or, "Is this project germane to the church's mission?" More free time for people does not give the church license to fritter it away with nonessentials.

The church is profligate with people's time when, under the impulse of various leisure-related factors, it espouses programs beyond its divine calling and competence. The field of psychotherapy is inviting to churches. In extreme cases it impels some churchmen with majors in theology and minors in psychiatry to exchange pulpits and altars for couches and counseling tables. To be sure, the pastor is a counselor. His counseling ministry extends to persons with emotional disorders. It deals with guilt, anxiety, compulsiveness, and despair. In instances when patients are treated by physicians and professional psychotherapists, the pastor continues as a member of the healing team. He makes his distinctive contribution to the patient's well-being when, as William E. Hulme stresses in *Counseling and Theology,* he ministers and counsels through the Word and the sacraments. It is quite another thing when the church and its staff leave the means of grace to dabble in the treatment of psychoses by skills not properly mastered. It wastes people's time and money when it sets up shop on church premises for the practice of an amateur psychotherapy for those who sicken of too much leisure. A ministry is necessary in these cases, but let it be the ministry of the Word, and let clinical problems be handled by specialists.

The growth of leisure bids the church remember that it is none of the secular institutions it often imitates. To focus on another area of alien preoccupation, the church is not an athletic club, with built-in bowling alleys, swimming pools, and other recreational facilities on a scale that would suggest a downtown YMCA. The church errs when it overlooks the means of grace in its sanctuary and instead enlarges the borders of its house by creating a larger play area. Extensions of parish programs and facilities which divert from the church's spiritual mission are unworthy approaches to a leisure culture.

Assessing the Facts of Leisure

To extend its ministry effectively to people in a leisure society, the church is well advised to undertsand the implications of new factors at work and to address itself squarely to them. If it receives signals from the surrounding world, it will know what shifts in culture values are taking place. An important shift involves the change from a work culture to a leisure culture. In the former, emphasis rested on the worker's participation in the production of goods. In the latter the erstwhile worker becomes a consumer of mass-produced things. A work culture is identified with a proletarian stress on the virtue of toil. A leisure culture calls for an interpretation of life which relates the worth of man, not to his working capacity, not to his prowess as a "steel-drivin' man," but to the truth of his creation in the image of God, his personal talents on many levels, his creative services, and his calling to enjoy his Creator and the works of His hands.

Having come to understand how a leisure culture turns the mores of an inherited work culture upside down, the church can come to grips with the new order and minister to it effectively. Its programs of worship and parish life may have to undergo readjustments in keeping with the options God grants His church in these areas. The changes will not affect the church's spiritual aims or the efficacy of the Word and the sacraments. What is involved is changes in methodology and strategy.

The church in the age of leisure will follow people to where they are, as it has always done. If on weekends people congregate at lakesides, Sunday worship in this environment is indicated. Of course, more than the usual drive-in theater-type preaching services, with their inevitable hit-and-run qualities, will be needed. The church will have to prove itself in these unstable surroundings as in all respects the body of Christ. It will be forced to find formulas enabling it to be a fellowship of concern among the unconcerned, to offer full ministries to people whose memberships are in congregations "back home," and to effect, more in terms of function than form, a program of continuity among perennial transients. In its "settled itineracy" status and amid the absence of the usual crutches of institutional Christendom — the "fortress" stone edifice on the corner of Third & Elm, hard and fast membership rolls, parish traditions — the church in the centers of leisure activities will be compelled to rely more heavily on the Word, and in that reliance find greater strength.

Meanwhile, in the parish back home, there may have to be an intensification of midweek worship services, and parish programs planned for days other than Sundays. The vacation Bible school idea, until now restricted to children in the summer, may develop into learning situations also for adults, and that on a year-round basis. In short, a church program based on the traditional week-plan of our culture: six days of work and one day of rest, will, most likely, give way to a new ratio of, perhaps, three days of work and four of leisure. The outcome may well be in the church's favor. As God multiplies the days of rest, there may be more frequent midweek participation in worship and the church's work.

Besides finding out where the people are on weekends and during other leisure periods, the church cannot escape its responsibility to discover more things about leisure. It will have to assess the many kinds of leisure and determine how they affect people. It will need to ask: What kind of leisure keeps people at home and what kind takes them to marinas, resorts, and other places away from home? What effect has leisure on individuals and on home life? In *The Church in the World* Richard R. Caemmerer writes: "Modern life, with its crowding in cities and the tensions of industry, has thrown additional strains upon the home. The old folkways and practices of finding recreation and cheer in the family circle have succumbed to commercialized amusement." Will the leisure age accentuate this trend or reverse it? Whatever the outcome, the church will have to continue its search for strengthening its ties with persons living under many circumstances.

The church needs to articulate its concern about the many conditions under which people encounter leisure and the extent to which they have free choice within the the whole context of "free" time. Not everyone who has leisure chose it. The free-time problem at this point intersects with the unemployment situation. Many persons, especially unskilled or common laborers, are idle much against their will, and consequently do not enjoy their leisure. Seasonal and migratory workers chafe under the problem of on-again—off-again employment. There are also the semiemployed, and these may include members of minority groups and the physically handicapped. The church wants to know under what conditions people have free time, whether it is voluntary or involuntary, and what remedial measures can be taken.

The church's appraisal of leisure facts ought to extend also to persons who are partially or totally reduced to involuntary leisure by reason of illness. These are patients confined to nursing homes, sanitaria, mental hospitals, psychiatric wards, and the inmates of prisons. In taking account of people in these circumstances of enforced leisure, the church is better able to direct its ministry to their special needs and aid them in converting pointless time into purposeful time.

The Church and a Theology of Leisure

The church assists its members in coming to a better understanding of leisure. Such assistance is necessary, since in the popular mind leisure is subject to distortions. Two extreme positions can be said to characterize leisure misconceptions: a free-wheeling libertinism and a moralism inducing guilt feelings.

The libertine view of leisure finds expression in dissolute and uncontrolled acts to which human nature is prone by reason of its base instincts. In apostolic times, Paul noted the unrestrained misuse of leisure in the amoral atmosphere of Greco-Roman society. His catalog of vices in Galatians 5 enumerates various forms of common immorality, including party-time "drunkenness, carousing, and the like." In the next chapter the apostle refers to this whole messy behavior as sowing to the flesh. He designates the inevitable harvest of such sowing as corruption. The frightening thing about Biblical portrayals of the works of the flesh is that they, despite their antiquity, are so up to date. What human nature was then it is now. The misappropriation of leisure for licentiousness is today as it was then. Give or take a little, there is nothing new under the sun.

On the far-right wing of leisure distortions is a nagging moralism stemming largely from the Protestant work ethics and issuing in a rigid, dour, exclusive "work and pray" philosophy. It leaves no room for the enjoyment of leisure in that it schedules time tightly for work. It seeks to derive its Biblical sanction from select texts commanding labor, but overlooks other texts which bless man's rest, reflection, and enjoyment of God amid leisure. It brands on men's consciences the words of God to Adam: "Cursed is the ground for thy sake. . . . In the sweat of thy face shalt thou eat bread," but forgets the blessing of God on spiritually reconstructed mankind: the divine blessing of rest in Christ, the Second Adam, and the enjoyment of everything this rest affords this side of heaven. Because of the incompleteness of such moralisms anent the work-leisure aspects of life, many people with religious upbringings find it hard to be creatively and recreatively at ease during uncommitted hours.

The passage to a viable Christian theology of leisure leads somewhere between the Scylla of libertinism and the Charybdis of a do's-and-don'ts moralism. The distance is considerably narrowed when Christian liberty is substituted for libertinism and Christian worshipful response for compulsiveness. Within the framework of Christian liberty and Christian response is a sufficient area for the development of a Biblical theology of leisure.

How is such a theology to be evolved? It is helpful to let a little of the methodological scaffolding show through. We said earlier that Pieper, speaking out of the context of a European synthesis of Christianity and culture, posited culture on leisure, and leisure on worship. By worship he means cultus, or the full system of religious rites and festivals. On the American scene, it is perhaps better to say that *in the future* our culture will rest on leisure, and that for Christians leisure rests on the sense of vocation rather than formal worship. Christian vocation — the spiritual priesthood of believers — is a broader concept. It conceives of cultic worship as a part of the total worshipful response of Christians to all that God has done for them in Christ. "Worshipful response" includes everything a Christian does in faith, and not only his cultic acts.

Christian vocation is a sound base for the development of a theology of leisure because it embodies the truth of a divine calling. It is the calling to the God-pleasing use of all of life's God-given gifts in all situations. The divine gifts enriching life include time in general, leisure as a special kind of time, and things that enter into the Christian's use of free time. The very idea of leisure as uncommitted time suggests, according to the dictionary, freedom, convenience, ease. Leisure is thus a gift God has given us to *enjoy.*

A golden text for the theology of leisure is 1 Tim. 6:17. In this passage Paul bids Timothy to urge the rich to cease trusting in "uncertain riches" and to place their trust, according to the King James Version, "in the living God, who giveth us richly all things to enjoy." Other versions render Paul's words in much the same way: ". . . God, who richly furnishes us with everything to enjoy" (RSV); ". . . God, who endows us richly with all things to enjoy" (NEB); ". . . God, who generously gives us everything for our enjoyment" (Phillips).

The divine authorship, the abundance and all-inclusiveness of God's blessing are points to be especially noted. God is a Giver extraordinary. After giving life to man at creation, He initiated a series of givings in a special way by first giving Himself. God so loved the world that He gave His only-begotten Son for the life of the world. In Jesus Christ God gave Himself, not to condemn mankind, but to save it eternally by His Son. Now, the logic of revelation continues (and Paul in Romans 8:32 follows precisely such logic): If God gave His own Son, shall He not also freely give us all things? The reply, as Paul emphasizes it to Timothy, is decidedly in the affirmative: God "giveth us richly all things to enjoy."

"All things": this is all-inclusive. The gift of leisure is included. Consequently, in paraphrase the statement reads: "God giveth us richly all leisure to enjoy." It is not His purpose to vex or burden His people when He gives them leisure. The gift is intended for their delight and pleasure. In the exercise of Christian vocation, that is, as Christians go about being God's people in church and world, leisure is given them for enjoyment. All the things related to leisure: the books they read, the music they play or listen to, the scenic works of creation they view — let Christians enjoy them, for they are God's gifts.

The Theology of Leisure Implemented

But how enjoy the divine gift of leisure? It is at this point that the church turns its theology of leisure to practical ends. It helps people discover new, creative ways for the enjoyment of leisure. To the usual service opportunities in church: teaching in the Sunday school, ushering, and singing in the choir, it adds scores of others commensurate with the individual's talents and time.

There are practical methods by which the church goes from phrase to fact in uncovering and enlisting talent and leisure time. On the local scene, congregations can circulate a simple questionnaire to determine who has what talent, who has time on what days and evenings. The idea is not to meddle into private lives or deprive people of personal leisure, but to assemble data useful to the church in extending its ministry to all the people and inviting their lay ministry in return. Such a survey, particularly in large parishes, will bring relevant facts to light. It will tap heretofore unknown sources of manpower and woman-power. The results might show that a group of men is available every Wednesday for specific kinds of services, that a dozen or more pensioners can give afternoons for worthwhile church work, that a score or more women whose families are raised are prepared to make home visitations.

Beyond services in and to the parish, the church's ministry to people in a leisure culture seeks to help individuals to a more enjoyable use of free time in their private lives. It aids them in relating their interests in education, the arts, writing skills, drama, human-relations work, and the like to Christian vocation. Through its existing Bible-discussion programs it encourages deeper soundings in lay theology, believing that the Word of God is the ultimate source of guidance for the enjoyment of leisure. The church cannot propound neat "how to" formulas to cover all instances of the right use of talent and time. But it can hold forth the right principles. It can instill a more profound appreciation of blessings shared through fellowship in the church as the body of Christ. As this appreciation grows, leisure problems turn to leisure opportunities in a world where so much remains to be done.

The good estate of the church in the world, from the human side, rests with a better grasp of the mission Christ has entrusted to all members of His body. This mission comprehends the right use of leisure also, to the good of church and human society at critical points in their history. It is as Howard Hong has stated in *This World and the Church:* "The hope of the world and the hope of the Church is in a reconsecration of Christians and the Christian Church to the Gospel of Christ who redeems, Christ who is the Lord of Life. Let God be God in eternity and in time, in His Church, in men, and among men!"

QUESTIONS FOR DISCUSSION

1. Explain what various meanings *leisure* can have.

2. In what respects is the present leisure different from the leisure of former times?

3. It is said: Quite often the wrong people have the most leisure. What is meant by this?

4. Look up Eph. 4:28 and 2 Thess. 3:10 to determine what the sin of idleness is. Why is the enjoyment of leisure not to be identified with sinful sloth?

5. How does the tendency to conform to mass behavior become evident in leisure-time pursuits? Do people also express individualism in leisure activities?

6. Explain how extra time and extra money combine to make expensive leisure pursuits possible.

7. How is the growth of leisure related to developments in the industrial world, such as automation?

8. In Eph. 5:16 and Col. 4:5 (King James Version) Paul speaks of "redeeming the time." How is leisure time redeemed?

9. Someone has said: "No Christian is ever off-duty for God." Does this mean that we should use all free time to pray and do church work? Does a Christian also serve God in his rest and recreation?

10. How can the leisure-time interest in drama, or the "little theater" movement, serve in the communication of the Gospel?

11. What is "Christian vocation," and how does it pertain to the Christian's use of leisure?

12. Should the church organize special "senior citizens" clubs or keep its elderly members active in the regular organizations, such as men's clubs, women's societies, and missionary groups? Can it be both?

13. What can people do now to prepare themselves for the use of leisure in retirement and old age?

14. What changes in organized church life may come as a result of more leisure?

15. In what ways can we help Christians use increased leisure as a gift of God?

FOR FURTHER STUDY

Pieper, Josef. *Leisure the Basis of Culture*. New York: Pantheon Books, Inc., 1961.

Kaplan, Max. *Leisure in America: A Social Inquiry*. New York and London: John Wiley & Sons, Inc., 1960.

Larrabee, Eric. and Rolf Meyerson, editors, *Mass Leisure*. Glencoe, Ill.: The Free Press, 1958.

Grazia, Sebastian de. *Of Time, Work, and Leisure*. New York: The Twentieth Century Fund, 1962.

Composed and printed by Concordia Publishing House. *Set in 9 point Times Roman, leaded 2 points. Printed offset on 70-pound Warren's Wove Publisher's White Eggshell. Designed by* Esther Carlson *and* Ted Smith.